Preaching the Story

Preaching the Story

Edmund A. Steimle
Morris J. Niedenthal
Charles L. Rice

FORTRESS
PRESS
Philadelphia

Library of Congress Cataloging in Publication Data

Main entry under title:

Preaching the story.

Includes bibliographical references.
1. Preaching—Addresses, essays, lectures.
2. Sermons, American.   I. Steimle, Edmund A.
II. Niedenthal, Morris J., 1931-   III. Rice,
Charles Lynvel, 1936-
BV4211.2.P73   251   78-14675
ISBN 0-8006-0538-1

7415F79   Printed in the United States of America   1-538

To Norman A. Hjelm
who encouraged this project
and to our students
from whom we have learned so much

Contents

Part Four: The Message

Part Five: Learning to Preach

Preface

Fortress Press initiated the preparation of this book by asking the three of us to produce a textbook in homiletics for seminary students which would also be helpful to ministers preaching in parish congregations. We have tried to do exactly that. As a consequence we expect that certain sections may be more useful to parish pastors, while other sections may be more appropriate for seminarians.

Morris J. Niedenthal, Professor of Homiletics at the Lutheran School of Theology at Chicago, and Charles L. Rice, Associate Professor of Homiletics at the Theological School of Drew University, are former graduate students of mine. The three of us share a common approach to preaching today, which is set forth in the Introduction and is implicit throughout the book.

There is much of course that could have been said in a longer or different book. More explicit attention might have been given to history and systematic theology. The abundant theories and studies of the art and science of preaching might have been considered at greater length. We have chosen to concentrate our focus rather on that one insight, or perspective, which the three of us regard as of high importance: preaching as storytelling and the preacher as raconteur.

We have asked other preachers to deal with some aspects of preaching which are related to our central concern. Gilbert E. Doan, Jr., Northeastern Regional Director, National Lutheran Campus Ministry, wrote chapter 5 on the liturgical context of preaching. Norman Neaves, pastor of the Church of the Servant (United Methodist) in

Oklahoma City, contributed chapter 6 on the pastoral context of preaching. Ardith Hayes, Associate Professor of Ministry, McCormick Theological Seminary, gave us our concluding chapter on women and the homiletics classroom. And two recent doctoral students in homiletics and New Testament, Thomas Herin and Ronald J. Allen, currently parish pastors in North Carolina and Nebraska respectively, collaborated in the writing of the chapter on hermeneutics, "Moving from The Story to Our Story." Although these colleagues share with the three of us our basic approach to preaching, it will come as no surprise that in matters less central than that of Story, they are not always of the same mind.

The whole venture has been a rewarding experience in collegiality for us. We submitted our material to one another for reactions and suggestions which were then incorporated into the final form of each chapter in turn. It is our hope that in learning to preach, the reader may experience a similar kind of collegiality with respect to other students, other preachers, and the listening congregation.

We have included a sermon to illustrate each of the first four parts of the book. Each of these sermons is to be studied as one way in which the authors' point of view might take sermonic shape. Our hope is that these sermons, by providing specific examples, may help clarify the text of the book.

EDMUND A. STEIMLE
   Brown Professor of Homiletics, Emeritus,
   Union Theological Seminary, New York City
   Adjunct Professor of Preaching,
   Wesley Theological Seminary, Washington, D.C.

Introduction:

Preaching as Shared Story

Morris J. Niedenthal and
Charles L. Rice

Books on preaching are written from markedly different perspectives. One perspective is suggested by the title of a book published not so long ago: *The Empty Pulpit.*[1] The author contended that preaching as it is commonly practiced is so ineffective as a form of communication that the pulpit might as well be empty. At about the same time, however, Gerhard Ebeling was arguing that preaching is both implicit in the gospel and essential to the life of faith.[2]

Could both of these writers have had the same phenomenon in mind? Yes and no. They were both concerned about preaching, but their perspectives were different. One wrote as a mentor of pastors, the other as a philosophical theologian.

In recent years preaching has been examined from many points of view — communication theory, psychology, and sociology, among others. This very multiplicity of perspectives has tended to obscure the nature of preaching itself and to confuse preaching with other kinds of communication. For those of us who are assuming the vocation of preaching in the church, what is needed is a holistic view which, although it makes full use of the critical insights of other disciplines, nevertheless values preaching as a unique activity and attends carefully to each aspect of it.

If we are to think toward a holistic view of preaching, four factors must be kept in mind at once: the preacher, the listener, the churchly context including the institutional organization, and the message. Any really comprehensive view of preaching must do justice to all four factors, without focusing unduly on any one of them. Part of the confusion in evaluating preaching today stems from the fact that there have been and are views of preaching which center in each one of the factors—and it is a very different view according to where it is centered.

One view of preaching centers in the person of the preacher, the woman or man called, trained, and ordained to the task. According to most exponents of this view, preaching is essentially *self-expression*. Phillips Brooks claimed that "preaching is the communication of truth by man to men."[3] Speaking of the apostles, he wrote that "when His treatment of them was complete, they stood fused like glass, and able to take God's truth in perfectly on one side and send it out perfectly on the other." And of that truth he wrote that it is "preeminently personal. However the gospel may be capable of statement in dogmatic form, its truest statement we know is not in dogma but in personal life . . . [and] must always be best conveyed through, must indeed be almost incapable of being perfectly conveyed except through personality."[4]

Truth was obviously a reality beyond the preacher but was often presented so vaguely that in the long run this view of preaching had the net effect of merely extolling the personality of the preacher. Carried to its extreme, this view makes of the preacher a prima donna, a religious virtuoso. Around the turn of the century some authors not only stressed the personality of the preacher but even used the elevated and romantic words *prince* and *king* to describe outstanding preachers and the word *throne* to describe the pulpit.[5] Today, these elevated expressions of prince, king, and throne seem clearly inappropriate and sound almost humorous. Nevertheless, preaching understood as self-expression is still current in forms other than the "royal" and has not lost its importance. It has even weathered the storm of the neoortho-dox revolution in theology.

Let us examine preaching in the context of neoorthodoxy; the movement raises a crucial question for preachers. Because it stressed the objective character of the Word of God, neoorthodoxy understood preaching as the self-expression of God rather than that of the preacher. An appropriate motto for the relation of the preacher to the activity of God in preaching was the cry of John the Baptist, "He must increase but I must decrease" (John 3:30). Preachers were advised never to refer to themselves or to use the pronoun *I* in a sermon. This intrusion of one's own person was thought somehow to obscure the pure Word of God.

Many preachers discounted this advice for several reasons. First, preachers are never neutral before the Word of God, nor should they be. Moreover, it is simply too easy, and at times too dangerous, for preachers to camouflage their own frustrations and self-expressions behind the sacred rhetoric. "The Word of God says . . ." Of all people, preachers should know that there is a fine line between prophecy and egotism! But third and most importantly, the fullest expression of the Word of God is in a person, Jesus the Christ, and therefore any view of preaching which depreciates the worth and value of a preacher's personhood is an interpretation foreign to the New Testament.

The crucial question, then, is this: can preaching be the self-expression of the preacher and, simultaneously, the voice of that Word which comes into the preachers' experience from beyond? Or to put the question otherwise, how can preachers maintain their own integrity as persons and, simultaneously, promise in ordination to teach and preach the Word of God in the Christian tradition? These are crucial and difficult questions which preachers need to face. There are no pat answers. Several suggestions, however, might prove helpful. Preachers must not transform the pulpit into a confessional booth where they vent only their own frustrations, disobedience, and lack of faith. Nor are they to take the pulpit to celebrate the virtue and strength of their own faith. As a listener in the pew, I have problems enough of my own without taking on the preacher's too, and the preacher's strong faith may serve only to complicate my own problems and compound my own guilt. The pulpit is not a confessional booth. Nor of course is it a platform from which preachers are free to propagandize for some of their favorite causes or projects.

Joseph Sittler presents a model for working through this issue of personal integrity and faithfulness to ordination vow in his sermon "The View from Mount Nebo" (see below). He recalls an episode in his preaching ministry in a congregation in Cleveland Heights, Ohio. He had been preaching through the Book of Philippians and had found the first part of chapter 1 well suited to his usual homiletical approach. Then he came to verse 21 of the first chapter, "For to me to live is Christ, and to die is gain." Sittler began his sermon that Sunday by saying, "I must declare to you something this morning that I do not know anything about." Since it made a considerable difference to him whether he lived or died tomorrow, Sittler could not bring himself to stand in the pulpit and say that it did not. Personal honesty and integrity demanded that he say no less. But personal honesty does not fulfill an ordination vow to be a preacher in the church. Sittler proceeded to speak of how God's grace had worked in Paul's life, that it had indeed made him so radically free that it made little difference to him whether he lived or died. Moreover, this same grace has the magnificent possibility of freeing a person radically here and now. Sittler had not yet experienced grace in this fashion. He might never. But Paul did and others have. By distinguishing between his own experience and the text, Sittler kept faith with the text, with his listeners, and with himself—and thus with his ordination vow. And his course of action bore eloquent testimony to his conviction that the Word is trustworthy quite apart from his own personality, experience, or attitude.

Preachers sometimes try to avoid the issue of personal honesty and integrity in preaching by talking of "the Christian." "The Christian is a person who is radically free. The Christian is a person for whom it makes no difference whether he or she lives or dies." This usage of "the Christian" sounds correct and proper, to be sure, but it allows preachers to evade the question whether living or dying tomorrow makes a difference to them. This approach leads to hypocrisy in the pulpit, and the church does not need it. The expression "The Christian is a person who . . ." should be used very infrequently in preaching, not only because nine times out of ten not even Jesus would qualify under the description given of a Christian, but also because it presumes that the gathered brothers and sisters are not Christian and can become Christians only as they measure up to the law and demand expressed in the description. In other words, no matter how earnestly preachers believe they are preaching the good news, their use of such statements as "The Christian is one who . . ." will usually have only a condemnatory effect. This question will be considered further in chapter 8 below.

Thus there is something altogether good and right about a view of preaching that centers in the person of the preacher: how, after all, could we even consider preaching with less than our whole self, our whole being? But it should also be clear that as a holistic or comprehensive view of preaching, it has some very serious liabilities and some dangerous flaws. Sociologically, preachers no longer hold the distinctive position in the community which they held a hundred years ago; they cannot assume that their status entitles them automatically to a hearing by a respectful public. And theologically, the Word is given to the whole church, not just to the preacher; it is the church which authorizes the preacher to declare the Word. Moreover, the preacher is the servant, not the master, of the Word. The Word preachers speak is not their own; they speak it only in the act of hearing it.

A second view of preaching centers in the people who listen to preaching, the gathered community or audience. According to this view, preaching is essentially *effective communication.*[6] Before preachers can know what to say or how to say it, they must know the people, their needs, their problems, their expectations, and their joys. Moreover, inasmuch as people live in a social and cultural context, preachers need to be aware of and knowledgeable about the way in which these contexts affect people, their cognitive levels, their value formation, and their symbolic and linguistic framework.

One interpretation of this view suggests that preaching should begin with the known problems and felt needs of the listener, should next clarify the problems, should then point to more fundamental needs, and should finally proceed to show how the resources of the Christian tradition meet the needs and/or resolve the problems. This kind of preaching is problem solving or need supplying. God, Christ, faith, and the Bible are means or resources for meeting difficulties as they arise. Christ is often spoken of as the *answer* to the problems mentioned. (One should remember that God and Christ are often spoken of as the *problem* in the Bible, and only when that is acknowledged and faced do they appear as friend or helper.)

A people-centered view of preaching is widely accepted today, especially among seminary students. And there is obviously something deeply right in it, namely that a preacher's relationship to the congregation and personal assessment of its needs provide a decisive focus for preaching to these particular people at this time and place. On this question see especially chapter 6 below.

There are however serious deficiencies in any view of preaching which is dominated by a people-centered commitment. Such views can be challenged on both psychological and theological grounds. Are preachers such fountains of wisdom that they can solve everyone's problems? Can any person's problems really be solved by somebody else? And in the question of need, who is to decide, who is to judge what people need most? The people? The preacher? The Christian tradition? Does the Bible not say some mystifying and disturbing things about what people need? How many people would agree that their most fundamental need was for forgiveness, repentance, and faith? Finally, do not people often refuse the thing they need most so long as they can divert their attention to the trivial things they *think* they need? For example, a person's deep anxiety might signal a fundamental need for a radical change in values or life-style. But such persons will often go to extraordinary lengths in their attempts to quell the anxiety, instead of facing and dealing with their more fundamental need for change—change such as the inbreaking gospel can bring about.

A third view of preaching centers in the churchly context and in its institutional form. From the institutional point of view, preachers are organizational people and their sermons essentially *promotion* or *persuasion*. Preachers preach the party line, imploring people to attend church regularly, to participate faithfully in the activities of the congregation, and to give generously to the work of the kingdom in the church.

Few seminary students and fewer seminary faculty members could probably ever see themselves adopting an institutional view of preaching. Many of them like to make sport of it. And yet the question at issue is too serious to laugh at. Many preachers, after they have been in the ordained ministry four or five years, come to accept an institutional view of preaching—often without being aware of the pervasive power of the institution in shaping the Sunday sermon.

Karl Hertz, writing on the sociological function and significance of preaching in a congregation, claims that preaching serves three purposes: to maintain and strengthen loyalties; to keep the Christian frame of reference intact, offering the perspective of life on God's terms; and to provide a therapeutic effect, giving people "something to go on" for the week. Hertz concludes that "good preaching, sociologically considered, brings people together, with all their needs, in order to express the relationships in which they stand and from which they get their meaning."[7]

A holistic view of preaching must take account of these sociological and institutional realities. We cannot make them go away by laughing at them, and if we do not think carefully about them they will likely become too conspicuous, too domineering. Despite the crass way in which the institutional view of preaching is often described, there is something right in it. The church, the family of God, is present in the activity of the congregation and in the activity of the church at large, and preachers cannot fulfill faithfully their calling to preach if they despise the church's operation in the life and work of the congregation. The notion that God is more interested in the preacher's sermon than in the activity of God's people is simply false. See chapter 6 below for a fuller discussion of this question.

A fourth view of preaching centers in the content or message of preaching. According to this view, preaching is essentially the *proclamation* of the gospel or of the Word of God. Gerhard Ebeling and many other professional theologians often write on preaching from a content-centered viewpoint. Some preachers are quick to agree. "That's it," they say; "that's what preaching is: the proclamation of the Word of God." Many seminary students today, however, are somewhat reticent to entertain such a lofty notion of preaching. Perhaps the truth lies somewhere between the views of the seminarians and those of the veterans. And perhaps the truth is not quite as simple as some veterans suppose.

Certainly preaching can ultimately be understood only within a theological frame of reference, that is, as an essential aspect of God's ongoing encounter with and address to his people and a pledge of his presence with them. The necessity of preaching in the Christian community is ultimately rooted in God's own self-giving activity, his own revelation of himself as witnessed to in Scripture, and in the response of faith to that revelation. Faith is "an acoustical affair," according to Luther; it comes from hearing the Word. The content of the message is clearly of enormous importance, as it reports and interprets the activity and action of God.

This is a day in which many persons clamor for action and for immediate experience. This clamor, or hunger, can sometimes obscure the need for the interpretation of such action and experience. There is a certain impatience toward interpreters who seem to some to "get in the way" of authentic, firsthand experience. But just as words without accompanying action are hollow and deceptive, so also actions without interpreting words tend to be ambiguous. The words of Jesus himself, for example, interpret his actions; his actions without his words would make him a mere enigma. Furthermore, Jesus was crucified not so much for what he did but for the interpretation he gave to what he did. He was accused of being a blasphemer. Moreover, his conflicts with the scribes and Pharisees frequently centered in his interpreting words. Consider his healing of the paralytic. The healing of the paralytic did not in itself arouse much antagonism; the hostility was evoked by Jesus' interpretation: "Son, your sins are forgiven. Get up and walk!"

The point is this: historical act and the interpretation of it are inseparable in the Christian understanding of God's self-giving. And so long as a Christian community exists (and there is no Christianity without the community), this activity of remembering and interpreting will continue.

In this sense, then, content-centered views of preaching are right. But these views too are partial and can be deceptive. It is simply too easy to say that preaching is the proclamation of the Word of God and then to dismiss everything else.

There are those however who preach as though the content of the message were the only consideration. And such preaching is often faulty in one (or both) of two ways. In some cases, preachers think their doctrine to be so high and pure, and its authority so sure, that nobody has to take the risk of believing or trusting God. The Word of God is given, they say, and that's that. Theology in such cases is often peddled monotonously as a formula of salvation. Such preaching has precious little self-expression in it, and it pays little attention to the listeners' need to understand and participate. The other danger is that preachers who are so much more concerned about the content of their sermon than about their listeners are inclined to speak to them in theological jargon which the listeners cannot understand. This content-centered view of preaching is the most difficult of all to unlearn.

Of the four partial approaches to preaching, then, each has its disadvantages and liabilities: the content-centered view tends toward incomprehensible jargon and toward a mechanization of the grace of God; the preacher-centered view toward egotism and subjectivism; the institutional view toward the promotion of something other than the gospel; and the need-centered view toward superficiality.

Yet each approach has its strengths: the preacher-centered view acknowledges the power of example, the importance of personal investment in interpretation, and requires honesty of the preacher. The need-centered view keeps the message "relevant." The community-oriented view takes seriously the family of God in ways that it is possible for other approaches to avoid, and the content-centered approach, in its very insistence on the truth, honors implicitly the God who is the truth.

But one cannot see—really see—a person's face by concentrating on eyes or lips or chin. One or another of these features may be a prominent or distinguishing—or dearly loved or unsettling—feature, but none, no matter how closely observed, *is* the face of the other. So with preaching. One can investigate intensively the preacher's life or the needs of the listeners or the dynamics of the community or the content of the gospel and still not lay a firm hold on *what it is to preach.*

Anyone who has experienced preaching, whether in pulpit or pew, knows that it is an event—a moment, a meeting, a sudden seeing—in which preacher, listener, the message, and the impinging social environment all come together. Can we find a word for that event, a paradigm which will recognize all the elements and in doing so tell us what preaching is, and how it is done when it is done well?

Ideally the life of the seminary might be such a comprehensive metaphor. Here are people who work and play, confront each other and share communion, and try to make ends meet while thinking about Augustine and the eschaton. The seminary is hardly a cloister any longer, and it would seem not a bad place at all to apprehend and communicate the tradition for our time. Theologians, we too easily forget, must struggle like everyone else with questions of vocation, identity, the needs of the world, and immediate personal problems, as well as with what Hebrews and Christians have said and done for thirty centuries. That is the setting and the makings of preaching, and not so different from the life of a parish church. Might we not reasonably expect lucid models of preaching in seminary chapels and even classrooms? Academic communities have after all called forth the best from such preachers as Tillich, Buttrick, Steimle, and Sittler. Even in sermon labs, despite video cameras and peer criticism, the Word *can* be spoken and heard. Sometimes the very difficulty and artificiality of the situation leads, by the sheer will to be open and attentive to others and to the Holy Spirit, to a real event of communication. See chapter 11 below on the possibilities for such a Word event in the classroom!

But all too often that does not happen, and we are tempted to go along with one of those appealing half-truths: "You know what preaching is by experiencing it in a 'real' situation," or "You learn how to do it by doing it." Almost any teacher of preaching, and surely many other experienced preachers, would agree on both counts and would agree that it is difficult for either to happen in the seminary. It is entirely possible for a student to give sermons for homiletics class, listen and speak to professors and peers in chapel, and graduate without knowing what it is to preach the gospel in a Christian community. It happens to scores of students every spring.

Perhaps Bonhoeffer was right in thinking that a critical, analytical attitude was not the milieu for preaching: the hearer's posture, he maintained, should be that of an obedient listener.[8] Today's seminaries may just be too analytical, not to say contentious, for the best nurture of preaching.

In fact theological education, when too narrowly conceived, can actually work against a holistic view of preaching and can in the end alienate from each other the preacher, the message, and the people. When a seminarian speaks of his parish assignment as "those people out there," he betrays an attitude which comes too easily from doing theology for theology's sake: the cook becomes preoccupied with the recipe. When that happens preaching loses its necessary connection with the life which preacher and people share, and sermons are given in much the same way that many term papers are churned out.

It is not unusual for seminarians to be threatened by preaching classes. And that is at one level easily understood. Who would relish preaching under lights to professor and fellow students, knowing all the while that the sermon was going to get some kind of criticism? But the threat is more profound. The sensitive student intuits that it is just here, in the attempt to bear personal witness to the gospel, that one's theological studies, one's experience in church and society, and who one is as a person must come together. Thus the promise of preaching is also its threat, for this is not just another academic assignment. In the necessity to preach, the deep ravines which separate person/message/preacher appear to the student as questions about role/identity/experience/tradition/life in the flesh with other people, and faith in God. Could our very anxiety about preaching tell us something important about what a sermon is, its theological basis, and our personal stake in it?

We suspect so. We hope so. And a first step in discovering the message of our anxiety would seem clearly to lie in determining what at bottom we believe preaching to be. Each of us needs (and has) a *model* for preaching. That does not mean that we each have a person to imitate, though a good personal model is always helpful. The preacher in the making (or remaking) needs a model of another kind: a model in the form of an *image*. The picture we have in mind, or "in ear," of "preacher" will mold each sermon we give. What model of "preacher" are you carrying around, consciously or unconsciously? Are you in fact hung up on a model? Do you measure yourself by a stereotype of *the* preacher? What picture would you draw of the preacher you would like to become? Does that picture correspond to or embody one of the *partial* views of preaching? Do you see yourself for example as a charismatic personality, or as an omnicompetent healer of hurts, or as the chief executive officer of a well-organized religious corporation, or as the guardian of the pure doctrine whose mere repetition assists, if it does not finally push, its listeners into salvation?

What is the *sound* of a sermon and who planted that sound in your ear? When you think of standing up in a pulpit to preach, who comes to stand in your imaginary vestry with you? Are those pictures and sounds blocking you from your own possibilities for serving the Word in your time and place and with your own unique gifts? As a first step on the track that this book will follow, try to get into touch with the preacher you are carrying around in your imagination and to discover if that caricature or actual person is a helpful model or a hang-up.

We are looking for a model that could free from stereotypes and be useful to students in seminary as well as to persons who have been preaching for a long time. And we need a model which does balanced justice to all four basic components of preaching: the preacher, the listener, the ecclesiastical and social context, and the message. Kenneth Boulding says that to a considerable extent our *primary images* make us what we are.[9]

We are trying, then, to find that formative image that could both articulate what preaching is and free people to do it. Is there an image adequate to shape the form, content, and style of preaching? If we had to say in a word or two, or in a picture, what preaching is and how it is done when it is done well, what would that phrase or picture be? Given the varieties of persons who preach and of the occasions in which preaching is done, is it too much to hope that a primary image could be found? If we could come up with one, it would almost inevitably begin to re-form much of our preaching.

Let us consider the storyteller. It is an image so commonplace in the Bible and so close in daily life as to be overlooked. We live by story, by the stories constantly being told and by the stories we tell ourselves. All sorts of less-than-valuable things are sold to us on the strength of their association in stories with what is priceless — our sexuality, our deepest fears and hopes, our affections. We look for that person or those persons with whom we can share our stories past, present, and future. We are forever getting caught up in subplots which drive us to try all the harder to connect with a larger, meaningful story which can help us to locate ourselves. We are preyed upon by people who know how to use stories to sell us a bill of goods (even from the pulpit!), and at Christmas we feel, despite the con stories, the power of a story told and retold from generation to generation. We feel lost when we forget the story which is peculiarly ours.

Story is so pervasive in our daily life that the word seems strangely nude when isolated in this way: story. We find ourselves wanting to add, "the story of . . ." or "a story about . . ." or most likely, to protest, "Don't talk about story, tell me one!" We resist because we know what stories are and how important they are.

As we relate to our families, to our own intimate past, to the people on our street or in our building, we connect each new experience to larger, ongoing stories. Discrete happenings are woven into a larger tapestry of meaning, our life story. At the most profound level of symbolization — where experience becomes meaningful — we relate our stories to The Story. If we were pressed to say what Christian faith and life are, we could hardly do better than *hearing, telling, and living a story*. And if asked for a short definition of preaching could we do better than *shared story*?

Picture, then, the storyteller—a listener, a host; grateful for language, for gifted words and metaphors, for the people who will enter into "once upon a time"; open to the moment and ready to meet it in freedom; loving the story, respecting its own life and its power, the people who have told it before or lived it; reliving the story in imagination even while telling it. See the storyteller in the middle of a circle of people; by the lake or around the fire; at the supper table on the evening of the funeral, over food gone cold and dishes unwashed; one to one, as the story comes out for the first, the healing time; over breakfast, with the newspaper open, remembering a little girl or boy; on the Fourth of July at a picnic, or at home on a snowy day with your grandparents; in a foxhole or a bar, or at the family reunion or around the communion table. The opening line is liturgical, a call to enter in and let something happen: "Once upon a time . . ." or "I remember when . . ." or "I've never told you this, but . . ." or "A certain man had two sons . . ." Wherever it happens and whatever the form, we recognize it immediately, and we begin, as W. B. Gallie has said, to *follow,* to go with the story and the storyteller,[10] whether the story is unfamiliar or one we have heard a thousand times.

When the signal is given, we know—and the knowing is simply a matter of our being human—that this is not a time to question, to analyze, to do anything. It is a time to lean forward, to enter in, to let ourselves be moved along, to follow. Paul Tillich's description of the moment when grace strikes us and of the need to let ourselves go could be an account of the appropriate response to a story's beginning.[11]

The storyteller and the circle of listeners *bend* to each other. There is in the very nature of storytelling a posture, a leaning forward. And this is true of both the listener and the storyteller, as if the story cannot be told without this attentive *bending* to each other. We have all experienced it in one setting or another. The story may be one we have heard before, and it may not begin with anything even resembling "Once upon a time." The storyteller may be friend and confidant; parent, preacher, or child; a neighbor—or even ourselves, when some object or word or odor or the way the light comes into a room in late afternoon recalls a time previously buried in memory. When the story comes, in whatever form, there arises in us such a need to live in and to live ourselves into the story that we bend our imaginations and, it would seem, our bodies as well to the storyteller. "Once upon a time" is a signal to pay attention to a discrete moment in time which can give meaning to all of time. Just as liturgical space—the naves, chancels, and altars which we set apart as holy—becomes the center of the universe to the bowing worshiper, so narrative can become a sacred time to which all our years and days are oriented. To put it another way, the stories we hear and tell and tell ourselves are our primary way of symbolizing, of turning into meaning what happens to us.[12] Just as liturgical postures show our awareness of sacred space and our need of it, so too the form of the listener bending intently to the storyteller is testifying to the truth that without the story, our history remains just-one-damn-thing-after-another, just as without the altar we get lost in both the city and the country.[13]

This bending of storyteller and listener is a matter of *speech*. This does not mean, of course, that stories can be told only orally; obviously some of our greatest storytellers are writers. Nevertheless, the essential form of storytelling is speech: one person asks for the immediate attention of another. This is the form in which the biblical stories were told, and it is in this way that most of the stories being told right now are unfolding. "Give me your *ear*," the storyteller says. That situation, speaking and being heard, is immediate; a person's voice is actually entering the ear of another person. Of course people do in fact talk past each other all the time, but however much that may happen, writing and printing can never hold the potential for immediacy that is in the spoken word. H. H. Farmer has shown that speech has the capacity for communicating such difficult ideas as law and grace, and their relationship, *at the same moment*.[14] What is being said is coming from a *person* who is being revealed in the timbre, tone, and volume of the voice as well as in the face and posture of the speaker. And all that is said is said within the context of personal meeting, of a shared moment, and of the possibility of saying more.

Anyone who has told a story knows that speech as we have sketched it here is the storyteller's medium. A good storyteller is bending to the circle, modifying the details of the narrative, perhaps adding to it, and modulating the voice for these particular listeners. Someone said that art is a lie which lets us see the truth. A good storyteller's story may change considerably from one setting to another; the New Testament provides plenty of examples. True, the story is there to be told; it has its own givenness. But it is not frozen there as in print; it is alive in the imagination of the storyteller. Where storytelling succeeds, the story becomes alive to the hearers as images in the mind's eye. Speech is flexible enough to bend spontaneously to the attentive circle so that the story can become shared story. Is it too much to say that the story, in the telling, is a *new* story which happens between storyteller and listeners who, all ears, bend to each other?

Perhaps the image of the storyteller can move us toward what we have called a holistic theory of preaching. What we hope for in the chapters that follow is the integration, in the sermons that our readers will give, of the preacher, the listener, and the message in the context of a Christian community. There is in fact some disadvantage in the format which we have chosen: it suggests that the preaching event is made up of component parts that can easily be diagrammed in terms of theories of communication. If we accept that at face value and begin to reify the diagram, then we fragment preaching. To isolate preacher, message, listener, and community from each other is to suggest that one can exist without the other, even to the point of assuming that the preacher "has" the message which is then "delivered to" the people. If we were to draw a picture of that, we would come out with something like a scene familiar to us all: a lecturer is reading a manuscript to a passive (or note-taking) classroom. We hope that the divisions of the book will not lead the student to think that speaker, listeners, community, and message exist—where preaching is concerned—apart from each other. That assumption could lead to the very polarization which needs to be overcome.

We hope instead that the image of the storyteller and the circle of listeners, bending toward each other in anticipation of the story which they share, will be seen to pervade each page that follows. And we hope too that this book will be used in the context of the actual doing of preaching.

Finally, preaching is shared story, and the vocation is learned best among people who share their stories and The Story with each other.

NOTES

1. Clyde Reid, *The Empty Pulpit* (New York: Harper & Row, Publishers, 1967).
2. Gerhard Ebeling, *Theology and Proclamation* (Philadelphia: Fortress Press, 1966).
3. Phillips Brooks, *On Preaching* (New York: Seabury Press, 1964), p. 5.
4. Ibid., p. 7.
5. Cf. Harry C. Howard, *Princes of the Christian Pulpit and Pastorate* (Nashville: Cokesbury Press, 1927); and E. Paxton Hood, *The Throne of Eloquence* (New York: Funk & Wagnalls Co., 1888).
6. This view dominates Clyde Reid's argumentation in *The Empty Pulpit*.
7. Karl Hertz, "Preaching is for Insiders," *Dialog* 3 (Winter 1964): 54.
8. For more of Bonhoeffer's views on preaching the reader should consult Dietrich Bonhoeffer, *Worldly Preaching,* ed. Clyde Fant (New York: Thomas Nelson, 1975).
9. Kenneth Boulding, *The Image* (Ann Arbor: University of Michigan Press, 1969), pp. 64–81.
10. W. B. Gallie, "The Historical Understanding," *History and Theory* 3, no. 2 (1963–64): 149–202.
11. Paul Tillich, *The Shaking of the Foundations* (New York: Charles Scribner's Sons, 1948), pp. 153–63.
12. Cf. Susanne K. Langer, *Feeling and Form* (New York: Charles Scribner's Sons, 1953). See especially chap. 13.
13. Cf. T. S. Eliot, "The Hollow Men" and "Choruses from the Rock," in *The Complete Poems and Plays* (New York: Harcourt, Brace & Co., 1952).
14. H. H. Farmer, *The Servant of the Word* (Philadelphia: Fortress Press, 1964). See especially pp. 37–65.

PART ONE

THE PREACHER

1

The Preacher's Story

Charles L. Rice

I once heard a preacher who sorely tempted me to say I would go to church no more. . . . A snowstorm was falling around us. The snowstorm was real, the preacher merely spectral, and the eye felt the sad contrast in looking at him, and then out of the window behind him into the beautiful meteor of the snow. He had lived in vain. He had no word intimating that he laughed or wept, was married or in love, had been commended or cheated or chagrined. If he had ever lived and acted, we were none the wiser for it. The capital secret of his profession, namely, to convert life into truth, he had not learned. Not one fact in all his experience had he yet imported into his doctrine. This man had ploughed and planted and talked and bought and sold; he had read books; he had eaten and drunken; his head aches, his heart throbs; he smiles and suffers; yet was there not a surmise, a hint, in all the discourse, that he had ever lived at all. Not a line did he draw out of real history. The true preacher can be known by this, that he deals out to people his life—life passed through the fire of thought. But of the bad preacher, it could not be told from his sermon what age of the world he fell in; whether he had a father or a child; whether he was a freeholder or a pauper; whether he was a citizen or a countryman; or any other fact of his biography. It seemed strange that the people should come to church. It seemed as if their houses were very uninteresting, that they should prefer this thoughtless clamor.[1]

Recall the image of the storyteller now, his listeners bending toward him, straining to catch his every word and nuance and holding their breath when he pauses. If what he says captures their imagination, it is clearly important to them that the storyteller *himself* be somehow reliable: that he not tell them something which would mean for them something radically different from what they heard in his last story; that he know and be at home in the things of which he speaks; that he respect the hopes and fears and values and common humanity of the circle around him; and perhaps most of all, that the story carry personal weight for him too. Certainly the story must be more to him than a way to exercise a contemptuous and manipulative control over his credulous listeners. In short, while there are many things the listeners do not need to know about the storyteller, there are some things of which they must be sure. Otherwise, he lacks that purchase on his listeners which enables the story to affect their lives — or even to secure their attention. The story is more than the storyteller, to be sure, but the voice we hear telling it is that of a *person*.

There was once a television entertainer, a storyteller; and there was once a father of small children. The children watched the entertainer regularly, and were enchanted by his stories. The father began to watch too. He enjoyed watching the delight of his children, and soon came himself to be captivated by the storyteller. Then one day the father met the storyteller on a train into New York and invited him to breakfast, eager to know him better. But to the father's disappointment, the entertainer talked almost uninterruptedly throughout breakfast not about stories or children but about unions, inner management conflicts, working conditions and pay scales, squabbles with associates — and all of it in a self-serving way. The father, in looking back on that morning, recognized that a professional entertainer high in the ratings might resemble only remotely the image projected by his program. For all that, however, he could never bring himself to watch the show again; he never heard the man tell another story.

All the more, then, we could expect that if the storyteller were the preacher rather than a professional entertainer of children, the listener would want to know *who* is preaching and how life looks to that person. That is a man or a woman up there in the pulpit; even liturgical overlay and pulpit manner cannot conceal that completely. Most of us are interested in *people* and what makes them tick, particularly if the person makes a vocation of talking to us about God.

As with our paradigmatic storyteller, the question arising from curiosity is mixed with the question of credibility: Does the preacher believe what he or she is saying? Is there any evidence in the preacher's life that the preacher believes what he or she is saying?

It is not that people allow no disparity between word and life; we clearly do. A faithful churchgoer, a Roman Catholic, said, "When the priest is up there at the altar, I don't care if he has ten wives hidden somewhere. As far as I am concerned then and there, he is the priest." As extreme as that may be, it is true to the *spirit* of Catholic theology, and there is health in it for the tit-for-tat legalist. There is a strand of Protestant theology in which it is understood that the truth of a sermon is tested and finally determined by either the piety of the preacher or the rigor of the moral code which he or she espouses. Neither of these positions—that of the sacramental catholic or that of the pious moralist—is an especially worthy representative of its respective tradition, but the extremes suggest the truth between them: God's Word comes because of *and also in spite of* us preachers, and we want at this point to inquire a bit more closely into the "because of." For just as in everyday speech people do expect some congruence of word and way of life, the sermon also is always heard in the context of the question, Who? Who says?

In addressing this question it will be important for us to steer clear of that narrow moralism which betrays a limited view of living and preaching: "Life is a simple matter of black and white, and the gospel tells us that we are supposed to be nice people." This is another of those half-truths, though in this case barely half. The preacher, in this way of thinking, becomes a moral arbiter whose function is to sanction morality and respectability. The preacher, in such a role, is obliged to exemplify the moral and social code of a particular community which that locality more often than not equates with Christianity: the preacher is expected to live in a small, provincial world (or in an urbane, supersophisticated but no less shortsighted one) and to be Exhibit A of its values and pieties. Notice it is more or less beside the point whether the congregation conforms to the code; that code may be no more than an idealized projection of what the congregation in fact is *not*. Where that is the case, a rigid double standard separates laity from clergy, and the pressure on the preacher may in fact increase. The preacher is expected to set an example and to "lay it on" the people for falling short of the standard. Imagine by way of a simple (and familiar) example a family with teenage children. The parents attend church and have firm opinions about who a minister is and how children should grow up—but are themselves, at bottom, high-living hedonists. The minister who calls on such a family will—quite typically — be asked to go down to the family room (where the television set is always on) to "have a talk with" the teenage boy who has been staying out late and refusing to go to Sunday school. How many ministers are playing just such a role when they stand up to preach? Clearly it will be easier in preaching to give free course to the Word and the Spirit if the preacher can be aware and steer clear of being forced into a role which serves primarily the congregation's sociomoral agenda — which agenda will often show up in an overweening curiosity about the preacher's own life.

In its healthiest forms, however, interest in who is preaching comes from the congregation's deep desire to "get it together" in their own lives. The more complex life becomes, the more people value any sign of wholeness and integration. "She talked straight" or "He spoke right from the heart" tells us what people listen for in the pulpit. People can fake it — and we preachers can fool even ourselves on this score — but sincerity scores high with most Americans. The barrage of commercial advertising, which we recognize immediately as a come-on and which we *expect* to be insincere, makes us value all the more the person in whom word and action match. Few people trust the political speeches of even our highest elected leaders, but most men and women would still like to think that the preacher both believes and lives what is affirmed in the pulpit. And when they listen to the preacher they will find it highly significant if the sermon and the life of the preacher are congruent.

It has been suggested that such congruency can play into the hands of a congregation's own sociomoral agenda. But it should be clear that congruency, if misperceived or overstressed, can also alienate the congregation. We are not called to be, in Updike's words, "exemplars of faith," standing in the pulpit to "burn them with the force of our belief."[2] If anything, the American pulpit has had too much of that: the completely assured and doubt-free preacher whose very confidence and optimism keep people at a distance and widen the gap between pulpit and pew. Robert E. C. Browne calls it "speaking smoothly of God," and Frederick Buechner asks if sometimes it does not appear from the storm-tossed pew as if the preacher were the only one who does not see that the waves are twenty feet high.[3]

There is a way of preaching which suggests that faith cancels out forever all pains and doubts, and purges from the human condition the sense of abandonment and of loneliness. Preaching of this kind however is ultimately alienating. People hearing sermons, Edmund Steimle has said, ought to be saying—or at least feeling at some inarticulate level—"That preacher knows what it is like to be me." That feeling can be evoked only by the preacher who does not forget what it is to be human, who knows that faith is forever in tandem with doubt, and who acknowledges that even in the highest flights of faithful proclamation we preach (to ourselves as well as to others) as to those who cry out, "Help my unbelief!" In that posture, vulnerable to the wrestlings which are the human lot, the preacher speaks not so much to as among the people, and the sermon can therefore move toward what Hans Küng hopes for: that condition in which "imagination finds expression in speech and is thus able to break down the crust which so often covers suffering, leaving it muffled, dumb, inarticulate."[4] To be a preacher is, in Küng's words, like being a Christian: it is to be radically human and to be unafraid to say so, because of a basic confidence that what God revealed in the Crucified is adequate for the whole of our lives.

It is essential, then, that the preacher address thoughtfully that hunger in the listeners to know who the *person* is who is doing the preaching. To be sure, the preacher must be aware that in some instances this curiosity represents a snare or trap which will make faithful preaching difficult or impossible. On the whole, however, if preaching is to affect human lives, it will clearly have to be done by someone who lives and preaches from a clearly human life—or it will not finally be heard except as entertainment or diversion.

It is not only the men and women in the pews who ask, "Who is preaching?" That is a burning question for the preacher as well. It can take many forms: Can I be myself and be a preacher too? Can I preach to people I do not really know or people who do not know me? What about my doubts, not to mention my weaknesses? (See below, Joseph Sittler's "The View from Mount Nebo.") How much of myself is it wise—or helpful—to reveal in the pulpit? Who am I to preach? Is not this the grocer's son? Am I not the salesman's daughter?

Such questions about role and identity are common among young preachers, and they ought to be seen as signs of health. For one thing, they show a proper humility in a brassy time! More importantly, such questions open the way toward integrating the vocation of preaching with a wholesome self-respect and sensitivity to one's own experience. Holding those together is the trick, and it is not easy to achieve.

Robert Raines, looking back over years as a successful clergyman and reflecting upon a more recent experience of getting into touch with himself as a person, describes a week in Maine with newfound friends:

> I had a week at Bethel to practice an alternative model of behavior, which for me meant saying no when I felt like it, looking moody when I was feeling moody, getting rid of the phony smile, being more honest in expressing my real feelings directly to people. I discovered that I had gotten out of touch with myself and had virtually disappeared into my role as a clergyman. I think this collapse into role or function, a kind of unconscious prostitution, is not uncommon for people in the helping professions—doctors, lawyers, teachers, and so on.[5]

The first call to preach raises a question which we would do well to keep on asking if we are to stay alive to ourselves and to the people around us: *Who* is preaching?

It is also a theological question. Karl Barth heard it that way and put it forcefully. He was, as he tells us, just out of the seminary and on his way one Sunday morning to preach in the small Swiss church where he was pastor. The ringing of the bells came to him as a question: "What is preaching? How *does* one do it? How *can* one do it?" (He spent the rest of his life on what he called a "marginal note" to that question, the *Church Dogmatics*.) How is it, Barth wanted to know, that the preacher's "own head and heart" serve the Word of God? It is a good question for any preacher at any age to ask: *Who am I* to preach the gospel? How can *I* preach? The person who can answer the question easily may well be someone whose personhood has been lost in the office of preaching itself. And the preaching of that person, by reason of that loss, dwindles to something less than the gospel demands.

Picture the person who has been preaching for twenty years, who has found a comfortable style and gives sermons week after week. "I am a preacher" comes easily, even glibly, as if it were the most common thing Sunday after Sunday to stand up and speak of God. How can that happen? Should it happen? And what actually has happened when the question is no longer there? This is a question that hits the young preacher hard and needs to be kept alive for all of us as long as we preach. Who am I to preach the gospel of Christ? Peter, no mean preacher, began with a demurrer: "Depart from me, Lord, for I am a sinful man."

Who is it that is preaching? If the question is urgent for the listener, it is equally urgent, or should be, for the man or woman who, though called, trained, and ordained, dares—*presumes*—to speak to others for God.

And how will the answer be made? In terms of each of two sides of an obvious reality: all preachers are human beings, which means that they have one characteristic in common—a life story which is unique. There is an answer which is obvious: preachers like everyone else are altogether human. And there is an answer which is no answer (or rather, which will differ from preacher to preacher): no one's life story is the same as another's. Let us look first at the first answer, namely, that that person who is preaching is a woman or a man and shares a common humanity with every listener. We all put our pants on one leg at a time, and being ordained does not alter that in the least. In fact, if to be in Christ and to give ourselves more and more to his service is to realize a fuller humanity and to participate more fully and freely in the life which he redeems, then to become a minister is not to be placed in a special class but rather to be with humankind and in the world more fully and unreservedly, and to move as openly and easily in the world as grace allows. Who you are and the way you live among your fellow human beings is at least part of the making of your ministry. Otherwise, why has God called *you*? Phillips Brooks, it will be remembered, thought that each of us is called to preach the gospel through the distinctive gifts of his or her unique humanity: God communicates through *your* personality.

We might however shy away from Brooks's dictum: "I am not interested in talking about myself." There may be those who want to be on parade, but to value privacy is to be human and healthy. Haven't we had enough, after all, of the "personality" in the pulpit? Preaching may be inseparable from who we are, but preaching is not putting ourselves in the limelight—or at least Paul didn't think so:

> For what we preach is not ourselves, but Jesus Christ as Lord, with ourselves as your servants for Jesus' sake. For it is the God who said, "Let light shine out of darkness," who has shone in our hearts to give the light of the knowledge of the glory of God in the face of Christ. But we have this treasure in earthen vessels, to show that the transcendent power belongs to God and not to us.   (2 Cor. 4:5-7)

If, however, we translate "personality" as "personhood," what comes into view rather than mere egotism is an open and honest humanity in the pulpit—a humanity which is not so far from Paul's image. Do not both the apostle and the preacher of Boston (as well as the listener in the church) want to see preachers whose earthy humanity is transparent to the gospel? Can we hope for that?

A humanity transparent to the gospel is not a matter of morality *or* of personality. And no more than the gospel depends upon our display of personality does preaching rest finally on what we are or on what we can achieve in and of ourselves. Who would want to argue—would even the most hard-nosed moralist?—that the shape of our lives could be congruent with Christ's? As W. H. Auden has said, the best Christ figures are those who by their *in*congruities show us by contrast who the Christ is. So we represent the Christ in the ne'er-do-well of *One Flew Over the Cuckoo's Nest,* the grotesque Joe Christmas, the clown, or in the preacher, whose humanness, like that of Graham Greene's drunken priest saying mass in a muddy hut, reveals God's grace. That should come as some comfort. Could we by stretching all our powers be the "exemplar of faith"? Perhaps a few might; and we can thank God for those sterling souls among us! They spur us on. But can we possibly justify ourselves as preachers by our moral or spiritual merits? Is the sermon God's word *because* it is the words of a pious and unworldly person any more than the bread and wine become to us the body and blood of Christ *because* of the priest's moral rectitude? A teacher of preaching—one of those Lutherans who know that one is justified, if at all, only by grace—counseled a student of his, "If you would give up trying to be such a nice guy, the Lord might be able to make something out of you!"

Being human serves the gospel. The more we feel free to be ourselves, to be with people, to be free to make mistakes and to fail, to celebrate small victories and to cry when the tears well up, the more we are likely to serve the Word of God. It is in those moments and to specific men and women that God's Word is always coming, where people laugh and cry, make it and fail, forgive and are forgiven, hope and fear. These are the words which describe life as we live it and liturgy as we celebrate it, and it is in that range of anxiety and joy, of falling ill and getting well, of being born and dying, that God addresses to us his Word in Jesus Christ. A large part of our vocation as preachers is to let ourselves flow more freely in the currents of human life, and to keep ourselves open to hear and speak the Word at the confluence of our stories and God's Story.[6] Even Barth started there, with what he called the "two magnitudes of preaching": life and the Bible. They come together when we believe deep down that God reveals himself, in the Bible and out of it, in the world of the flesh, in what happens in and to people.

Who then is this person who is preaching? First of all, a human being. And the preacher who gives to a listening congregation no convincing evidence of that shared membership in a common humanity is a preacher who has already forfeited any right to be taken seriously.

Strange as it may seem, however, translating this insight into homiletical practice can also be threatening, both to our congregations and to those of us who preach. How much easier it is—at least more manageable—to separate identity from role, pew from pulpit, and life in the flesh from figures in stained glass windows! Setting the preacher apart as a special sort of person—a Holy Joe or an unquestioned authority—is symptomatic of a much larger syndrome in the churches. For to see the preacher clearly as a human being would be to call the attention of many men and women to the broad and deep chasm between their daily lives and their Sunday morning goings-on.

Let us take as a particularly contemporary and sensitive example the ordination of women. Why is it a threat to so many churchgoers, not to mention preachers? Is it perhaps that the sight and sound of a woman in the pulpit, whether actual or imagined, confront us in a new way with the preacher as a person? We are so accustomed to men in the pulpit and to the style which acculturated males impose that a female preaching has a predictable effect: we see a *woman* in the pulpit. That forces us to face squarely the humanity of the person preaching. The very presence of women in formerly male territory makes unavoidable, for example, the sexuality of the preacher—as wife or husband, as father or mother, as lover. Could the ordination of women arouse such widespread anxiety if it did not touch us at the point of some deeply felt need to separate the preacher's humanity from the office of preaching? It is of course much easier for us to bracket a man's humanity when he functions in a role—whether as businessman, professional, even father—than to forget the personhood of a woman. But there is a good reason, sometimes unexamined, which makes it doubly difficult to cope with a woman in the pulpit. The reason lies in stereotyped sex roles long enforced by our society. Men, for one thing, are conditioned by our culture to keep emotions in, to be cool and commanding, that is, to suppress what would reveal them as persons. It is relatively easy therefore for a male preacher to be "simply" a preacher and not significantly a male. Women on the other hand have been asked to look sexy but not to be sexual persons—just the opposite of men. Small wonder, then, that the liberation of women and their presence in the pulpit threaten us! They oblige us finally to come to terms with personhood in preaching!

Could it be true, though, that in this threat there lies also a promise—the promise of a new freedom to speak and hear the gospel in a way that is appropriate to our time? Are there not large numbers of male preachers who have tried hard to live up to what is expected of them, and who in that attempt have suppressed their own personal stories? Do they not stand to experience an enormous liberation from the emergence of women into leadership in the church—leadership of a kind which is so patently human? Perhaps the presence of a woman in the pulpit—ironically enough, since a woman is the last person from whom many people expect to hear God's word—can help us to see that it is precisely through a person who is of the earth, with a full range of emotions and not only unafraid, but even required by the culture to be able to express them, that the lively word of God comes. (See chapter 11 for a fuller discussion of women as preachers.)

What is at stake, then, is the humanizing of preaching. What sort of person should a preacher be? Should the preacher share his or her experience in the pulpit? If so, how do we do that while remaining faithful witnesses of "the faith once for all delivered to the saints"? One answer is given among Joseph Sittler's questions in "The View from Mount Nebo." Let us consider another approach.

If we could draw a picture of the person we would want to preach to us, what would it look like? John Updike gives us two profiles of the minister; they are actually caricatures.[7] Eccles is the man about town, with it, uneasy with preaching, and most comfortable on the golf course or "rapping" in a small group. Kruppenbach, on the other hand, sees himself as a kind of white knight of faith and preaches so as to "burn people with the fire of his belief." Kruppenbach is more clerical in his undershirt mowing the lawn than Eccles in his vestments standing at the altar. When Rabbit Angstrom comes in to talk with Pastor Kruppenbach about his messed-up life, the pastor seats him on a church pew and tells him what's what. Eccles, by contrast, has little direct advice to give but seems to be both available and more or less chummy. Whatever else we may say about him, Eccles is *with* Rabbit: he lets him see the mixed foibles and graces which Rabbit sees in himself. He would qualify to some degree as both Kierkegaard's ironic knight of faith and Henri Nouwen's "wounded healer." But both Kruppenbach and Eccles are caricatures. It is in fact not easy to draw a picture of the ideal minister, but Eccles's personal style appeals to us.

Kruppenbach and Eccles and the matter of personal style will serve to raise the next part of our question: granted now that the humanizing of preaching is a matter of first importance both to the congregation and to the preacher, and granted also that to be human is to have a unique life story, how does that uniqueness, essential to humanity, find its way into faithful preaching?

A whole generation of preachers were trained to apologize: "Pardon a personal reference." How are we to account for this? For one thing, the manners of polite society teach us reticence about ourselves: "Tell people only what they need to know"; "A letter should never begin with the perpendicular pronoun"; "Fools' names and fools' faces . . ." The ministry in this country has been identified by and large with middle-class respectability, and WASPs, long the prototypical middle class, do not express their emotions or share their private experiences in public. (This may be due in part to the secretive behavior cultivated by affluent persons whose way of life depends upon making money, and who having made money exercise their influence on manners. Notice that envelopes containing checks are frequently marked "personal.") And as was noted in the Introduction, neoorthodoxy has left its imprint on preaching. Regardless of class, philosophy, or manners, however, privacy has a value of its own. Who is there that does not value it in one way or another?

There are at the same time, however, theological, hermeneutical, and practical reasons for bringing our personal experience—private and corporate—to the pulpit. And there are ways of doing so that do not force the listener to become an unwilling peeping Tom.

The Word of God, as we have said, takes human form. That is clear in the Bible, which is in large measure the story of people, people on journeys, failing and being restored, getting lost and being found, hoping for new land and remembering another time. If we take our cue from the Bible we can hardly talk about God apart from our own experience. It is likewise with the church, which through its long history has held out for the humanity of Jesus Christ: in the man Jesus we see God. Does it not follow, then, that it is precisely human personality and human words which will carry the message today?

It will be necessary at this point to exercise some fairly relentless intellectual self-discipline. The point has been made that it is necessary to distinguish the human being from the preacher. The ordination of women has brought the question sharply into focus, and the caricatures of Eccles and Kruppenbach have underscored it. But it is not enough to provide, in the sermon, material about the human race; it is necessary rather so to deal with these materials as to make it plain that one has lived, as fully as the preacher, in the flesh.

Phillips Brooks addressed this question rather pointedly. He wanted, he said, to get rid of all "undue solemnity" which turned a person into a *preacher,* and he spoke out on that precisely because of the doctrine of the incarnation. Preaching regularly, Brooks thought, could lead to a habit of mind—he called it "criticism"—which keeps us from really giving ourselves to experience: we stand aside and "criticize" and assess the serviceability for our professional tasks of the world around us. We refuse to allow ourselves to be taken over, even overwhelmed, by experience as by sex or a summer storm. This detached attitude leads to a kind of perverted professionalism— Brooks called it "mechanism"—which manipulates experience rather than honestly entering into and sharing it.

So also for us: we are often tempted to *use* what happens to us in our service of a prior agenda: the making of sermons. When used in this way, however, the human stories become merely professional anecdotes, sermon illustrations. Such illustration, however, often functions in the sermon as a way of avoiding such real experience as is genuinely organic to this time, this place, this congregation, this preacher. A snappy sermon-starter may actually distract and distance preacher and people from experience and from each other. These illustrations may be lofty accounts of people so saintly as to be unrecognizable by ordinary mortals, or stories of the most extreme situations: they come across as remote and irrelevant. Or they may be stories from daily life or from the Bible—what a storybook!—which are so dressed up for their appearance in church that we cannot imagine their happening to real people. In either case the artificial, prettied-up stories are but a stand-in for the shared human story, and the result is a sort of homiletical Docetism.

Two seminarians preached in Sermon Lab. Mary spoke (and it may be significant that the preacher is a woman) on "Jesus the Unexpected." She chose to use the audio room. The sermon began with a story about the unwary in the big city "putting his foot in it" and moved on to a selective exegesis of Mark 8. Exposition included Advent motifs but relied principally on Mary's recent experience: her frustration during a classroom discussion on Christology; her relationship with a Jewish pediatrician frustrated by the politics of their community; the ups and downs of being a wife, mother, and student. Mary's way of speaking—her usual speech with perhaps a pinch of ginger—would have been right for her kitchen or the classroom. Vocabulary and idiom owed as much to the lingo of Mary's teenage children as to the university. The sermon was whole: Jesus the unexpected, coming unexpectedly into a young woman's life and coming into a young woman's commonplace stories, in the context of biblical exegesis. It was, I suppose, important for my hearing of the sermon that Mary had been to my office a couple of weeks before to talk at length about the very christological problem which lay behind the sermon; I was aware of some significant theological reflection behind it. But when it came to the sermon it was Mary and her world that came through. Mary is new at homiletics.

John, by contrast, has been preaching for several years. He chose the chapel rather than the audio room, and elected to wear an academic gown. Like many of us who grew up in the church, he has embedded in his psyche a certain preconception of preaching as a feat. Given that notion of sermon giving, John gives sermons very well indeed. His sermon (he called it an address on the title page), "What Do We Do with Fear?" was polished, orderly, thoroughly logical, and well illustrated, as we say. John spoke of the universality of fear, even of its positive contributions, and then with real dramatic ability admonished us to faith and courage by pointing to the story of Jesus calming the storm at sea and to such heroic models as Admiral Nelson and nurse Edith Cavell. I am quite sure that had John given his sermon in my class at seminary fifteen years ago he would have received an A.

But there was something missing from that sermon. It had to do with style (a factor which is much more than grammar and punctuation). In the course of his discourse—and that is what the sermon was—John spoke of "healthy fear": "I would hate to go into a hospital to have an operation by a doctor who wasn't afraid . . ." As the class sat in the seminar room responding to John's sermon, someone asked, "John, are you ever afraid?" As we talked, the consensus emerged: John had done a good piece of work, but his style was the problem. He projected the image expected of him, the enabled and confident preacher discussing various ways of dealing with fear. Never imposing his personality upon the material, he stopped far short of that experience suggested by the gospel song, " 'Twas grace that taught my heart to fear, And grace my fears relieved." How could a listener trust what John said about fear, since John had given no evidence of having himself been afraid?

So it is, then, that the preacher can learn how to be a personality without ever being personal. When the success of the church, even of the gospel, is thought to depend upon the projecting of an assured, confident, almost omniscient image, the ministerial result is the vivid personality who seldom appears as a person, least of all when preaching. And that result is, simply, incredible.

The personality without personhood appears at every level of the sermon. The content is likely to be either discursive or at the other extreme cheaply emotional: they are two sides of the same coin. The discursive style evades human experience, and superficial emotionalism parodies the human situation. The delivery is likely to be stereotyped, which is another evasion. The preacher is apt to rely on canned illustrations; slices of human life are seen as lines for a performance rather than as the very locus of the incarnation—as if the purpose of living were to make sermons! And the result is pat, glib, and dead.

It is not an unusual pattern, either in preaching classes or among seasoned preachers, to see human life so abused by its reduction to fodder for a speech. The experiences which could give rise to our best preaching and provide its affective sources are buried by role expectations and by our habits of living and thinking.

There is however a homiletical style which is more in keeping with the way we actually experience life and discover truth. Fred Craddock has called this method *inductive* preaching.[8] This method, both in preparing and delivering the sermon, begins where people are. It starts with experience and then moves toward Scripture and tradition. That way of going about it would help John, so that he does not get lost so easily in the role of The Rev. Mr. So-and-So. Rather, from the outset, he must establish himself with his hearers on the basis of experience which he must identify so accurately that the listener has confidence in him and sees the value of continuing to listen. If this confidence is lost, the listening is only formal and the Word is not heard. If he is dealing with fear, for example, John may have to admit that he has himself been afraid. And he may even have to tell a story that persuades his hearers that he knows what fear is. Let it be clear: what is proposed here is a very different thing from navel gazing in public. There is no question here of privacy invaded. Taste, self-respect, and a sense of what is appropriate should guard us against using the pulpit as a place either to hang out our dirty linen or to expose to public view what other people have confided in us.

"We preach not ourselves . . ." to be sure. But the treasure we have is contained in very earthen vessels, and it is in *our* very human hearts that the light of God has shined. If our commitment is to see that light shine in other very human hearts, we had better not pretend in handling the treasure that we are made of anything other than the same "earth" of which Paul spoke. This may be the heart of the matter: we want to serve the gospel with all that we individually are here and now, and in a way that points beyond what we are here and now. That is no small matter; in it lies *the* question for homiletics, and from it come the crucial decisions for every sermon we will preach. So we want to know how to live in the flesh in a style which can carry the gospel easily from life at home and around town to the pulpit. As Auden has it,

> A poet's hope, to be,
> like some valley cheese,
> local, but prized elsewhere.[9]

Would Kierkegaard's "knight of faith" be a good model for the preacher? He enjoys walks, his neighbors; he looks forward to his supper and his pipe; and he is as unabashed about loving the earth and enjoying life as he is unpretentious. Is it possible to be provincial, in the best sense of the word, but also a citizen of the "global village"? That is probably the sort of person we need in the pulpit these days, someone who is unequivocally local but who is also in touch both with a wider world and with the tradition of catholic Christianity — and this raises the question of a larger story.

Most people try to connect their smaller stories to a larger one; there is hardly a tribe in the world that does not ritualize the significant events of the human story in a way which ties them to the processes of nature and the rhythms of the universe. It is the same in the church. At our baptism we enter into a story, a very large one; call it The Story. From that time we mark liturgically the significant moments of our life—coming to puberty, marriage, the birth of children, death—and we mark those moments in ways that relate them to The Story. The central events of Christian worship and of the church year reflect and recapitulate the course of our life cycle — and the course of The Story. At the center of all is the integrating symbol of our faith, a story: the life, death, and resurrection of Jesus Christ. That story itself is in the context of another story, the history of Israel, and it is a symbol competent to touch our life stories in all their heights, depths, and diversity. Our stories merge with The Story, find their meaning in that coalescence, and if we allow it, renew the telling of The Story.

When we speak, then, of preaching as shared story, we are not proposing the telling of stories which could hide our real lives or which would substitute for the biblical story. We are not talking about fairy tales, canned anecdotes, or snappy sermon-starters. Far from it. Sermon as shared story makes a place for each of our stories to make contact with and to be integrated into the stories of the Bible and of other people. Isn't it true that people begin to listen when someone says, in effect, "Something happened to me?" And isn't it also true that we begin to hear the Bible, really to hear it, when we come to the stories there expecting them to connect with our stories, with what we are going through now? P. T. Forsyth once said that the cure for boredom in the pulpit is not brilliance but reality. And is not faithful preaching exactly that which through the genuine humanity of the preacher's own story is able to connect the hearer's human story with The Story?

And we might add, preaching as shared story helps us to stay in touch with our own individual stories. An earlier generation of Americans kept diaries: everything that happened was important to God, they believed, and it was therefore important also to them. If we believe that the Word of God continues to come in some way that is analogous to the Word become flesh, then the life we have together with all God's creatures becomes the place of his continuing revelation; the realm of creation, as Emerson intimated, is the arena of redemption. Preaching as shared story is the event in which our particular stories are caught up into The Story to be judged, redeemed, and enlarged in purpose. And when, in order to share the story, we share with the community of faith who we really are as human beings—and that takes courage, not bravado but courage—The Story appears in what Walter Wink has called "a communion of horizons."[10]

There are, of course, many ways of being a preacher. Some of the ablest have been men and women about whom we could learn very little by reading their sermons, except that they took Scripture, theology, and people seriously. There is no reason to fault them for that. There is surely something majestic about a preacher standing up in the pulpit and, in the language of the Bible and of Zion, telling us what's what without paying too much attention to our mundane life together. But it is increasingly difficult to imagine such a preacher.

Perhaps it is the spirit of our times: a new personalism, a predisposition to informality, a habit of instant intimacy. Or it may be that the media have so altered our ways of sending and receiving messages that we now have to participate if we are to communicate. For whatever reason, however, we are less willing now than even a few years ago to accept the minister as a professional like any other professional.

The preacher today must share with the listener not merely certain professional transactions but his or her life, both in living and in speaking. For a society characterized by a certain reserve, to be sure, such sharing will have its threatening aspects. But for all that, a ministry—and preaching—which are both faithful to Scripture and responsive to the mood of the present day are personal investment, and will no longer be received unless they are clearly that at least. And the preacher who knows what it means to live by the grace of God will be able to make that investment.

NOTES

1. Ralph Waldo Emerson, "An Address Delivered before the Senior Class in Divinity College, Cambridge, Sunday Evening, July 15, 1838," in *Complete Works of Ralph Waldo Emerson,* 12 vols. (Boston: Houghton Mifflin Co., 1903–4), 1:127–51.

2. John Updike, *Rabbit Run* (Greenwich: Fawcett Publications, 1960), p. 143.

3. Robert E. C. Browne, *The Ministry of the Word* (Philadelphia: Fortress Press, 1976); and Frederick Buechner, *Telling the Truth: The Gospel as Tragedy, Comedy and Fairy Tale* (New York: Harper & Row, Publishers, 1977).

4. Hans Küng, *On Being a Christian* (New York: Doubleday & Co., 1976), p. 578.

5. Robert Raines, "A Revolution of Understanding," in *What's a Nice Church like You Doing in a Place like This?* ed. Wayne Robinson (Waco, Tex.: Word, 1972), p. 124.

6. See James A. Sanders, *God Has a Story Too: Sermons in Context* (Philadelphia: Fortress Press, 1979).

7. Updike, *Rabbit Run.*

8. Fred Craddock, *As One Without Authority* (Enid, Okla.: Phillips University Press, 1974).

9. W. H. Auden, "Short I," *Epistle to a Godson and Other Poems* (New York: Random House, 1972), p. 37.

10. Walter Wink, *The Bible in Human Transformation* (Philadelphia: Fortress Press, 1973).

2

By What Authority?

Edmund A. Steimle

The perplexing problem of the preacher's authority is rooted in our understanding of the nature of preaching, of what really is going on when a preacher gets up in the pulpit and preaches a "sermon." And there is considerable confusion, in the minds of the listeners at least, as to what really is going on during the preaching event. For example, as I like Job's Satan go "to and fro upon the earth and walk up and down upon it" preaching hither and yon, the reactions at the church door afterwards indicate a good deal of confusion among the listeners. "I enjoyed your talk," for instance. Well yes, I suppose it was at least that, a "talk." But the sense of authority conveyed by the word *talk* is surely minimal at best. Or "Thank you for the message." And the word "message" conveys about as much authority as a TV commercial: "Stayed tuned for this interesting message." Is a sermon a commercial, a plug for God?

And then there's that dear soul down South somewhere, whose total reaction to my sermon that morning was, "You ought to have your mouth washed out with soap and water." Certainly that sermon had no authority for that listener.

Of course, preachers and theologians have not been at a loss for theological answers to the question, What is preaching? Phillips Brooks, as we have seen, contended that preaching was the mediation of truth through personality. And that seems to me to be both too broad and too limited at the same time, and it also, unfortunately, fed the cult of the "great preachers" of the nineteenth and early twentieth centuries, whose designation as princes is not easy to square with the call to be the servant of the Word. Homiletical authority, such a designation clearly implies, is vested in the personality of the preacher. In contrast, Karl Barth said, "Preaching is the Word of God which he himself has spoken."[1] For Barth, clearly, there is no question about the preacher's authority; it is that of the "Word of God." But how is a preacher to determine the difference between his words and the Word of God? Surely there is a distinction. Moreover I question whether there are many congregations left today who listen dutifully and reverentially to their minister's sermon as "the Word of God which he himself has spoken."

Almost all preachers and theologians, including myself, accept the definition of preaching as "the proclamation of the gospel." But the word *proclamation* presents problems. For one thing, it suggests an activity much too formal, like the president's Thanksgiving proclamation. And it is too remote. It suggests a king's herald standing on a hilltop, far off and high up. It sets the preacher apart from and above the congregation, talking down to the people rather than with them. I understand the preacher to be simply one member of the community of faith who is given biblical and theological training and is then called by the community (and ordained) to do on their behalf what the training has made it possible to do: to interpret the biblical story in terms of their world and their stories. The preacher does not preach at them but talks with them. The preacher is not above them. The most appropriate place for the preacher to stand is as close to the level of the congregation as possible, given the practicalities of being seen and heard. The size or height of the pulpit has little to do with the authority of the preacher.

The picture of a revival preacher, Bible prominently held up in one hand, is an image of the authority of the preacher. For what other authority is there than the Word which we proclaim, or The Story which we preach? Apart from the Bible in hand or the Word in mouth, what other authority is there?

But the question of authority is not so readily dismissed. What of the preacher's own life and experience? Sometimes what a person is speaks more loudly than what the person says. What of the preacher's own story? Surely the preacher's own experience of the faith has something to do with the authority with which she or he preaches the Word.

But personal experience takes us only so far. There come times when we are called to speak beyond our own personal experience. Every time we hold out the hope of an eschatological banquet in the future or the assurance of life beyond death, we speak necessarily of things beyond our own personal experience. Joseph Sittler's sermon "The View from Mount Nebo," which follows this chapter, is eloquent testimony to the occasional necessity that preachers speak beyond their own experience. So we are driven back to the authority of the Word itself.

But what of the authority vested in the preacher through the community of believers? What is the meaning of ordination—of being "called" by a congregation to preach the Word to them? Some lay persons are frankly amazed to learn how much responsibility is vested in them through the constitutional documents of a congregation, documents which require them to see to it that the Word is faithfully preached and the sacraments rightly administered. There is the fact that preaching is in a very real sense a congregational act, not just a solo performance by an individual. (See below, chapter 5.)

Is there for example a difference between a lay person's getting up in a pulpit to preach, Bible in hand, and an ordained minister getting up in a pulpit to preach a sermon based on a lection for that Sunday in the church year? And if there is a difference, what constitutes the difference?

Surely a lay person may well get up in the pulpit and offer personal witness to what the faith has meant to him or to her. But as we have already seen, witness to a person's own individual experience, though important, takes us only part of the way along the road to a biblical sermon.

Nevertheless, we need to pay more attention than we usually do to the vital place of the community of believers in the authority of the preacher. The office of preaching belongs ultimately to the community of believers, the congregation, not to the person of the preacher. The act of ordination, along with the examining process which normally accompanies it, is testimony to the fact that the office of preaching belongs to the community of believers. Indeed, the vestments we wear, whether black gown or alb and chasuble, bear visible witness to the fact that what is going on here is more than just one individual's own personal act, no matter how committed or personally sincere the individual may be.

All this was brought home to me some years ago when I was preaching in a seminary chapel which had no denominational affiliation. It was an Easter service and I was wearing the customary vestments of my denomination at the time: cassock, surplice, and stole. After the service and sermon, a student who belonged to a nonliturgical denomination came up to me and told me that he was impressed by the vestments (which were strange to him) because, he said, they pointed to the fact that this was not just Ed Steimle's personal witness to the fact of the resurrection but that it was the proclamation of the church to the reality and the implications of the resurrection. And he was right! Whenever I wear clericals — collar or vestments — it is with the self-conscious intention that my own personal witness is undergirded by the witness of the church which ordained me and to which I am committed in virtue of my ordination vows.

But prior to ordination I was trained in a theological seminary. And it is the community of believers who provide the seminaries for the training of ministers-preachers, precisely because of their concern for the authority of the Bible. The most practical courses a theological student can take in preparation for preaching are exegetical courses and courses in biblical studies. For this is what the preacher is called to do: to interpret the biblical story in such a way that light is shed on the stories of the community of believers and on the preacher's own story.

Indeed, when the preacher turns to commentaries and other technical aids in the interpretation of the text, the intent is to turn to the scholars of the church in order to make sure that the preacher's own personal interpretation of the text and preaching of The Story will be as much as possible the proclamation of the church as well as the preacher's own personal witness to the faith. Likewise, when the pastor in a congregation engages in continuing education programs and attends preaching workshops, the motivation is not simply to sharpen preaching skills but also to check the major emphases in the preacher's own sermons against the considered judgment of scholars of the church who are, again, provided by that community of believers which owns the preaching office.

But this emphasis upon the authority vested in the preacher by the community of believers does not rule out the possibility that preachers in their prophetic role may speak against the community of believers. Were this not so, there would have been no Luther or Wesley, no

Protestant Reformation, nor the possibility of the ongoing ref
tion of the church today.

But when preachers assume this prophetic role, they do not enter
into it lightly. They do it on the basis of conscience illuminated by
Scripture, not in the heat of anger or frustration.

Moreover, preachers will never fail to identify themselves with that
aspect of life in the community of believers against which the prophetic
Word is proclaimed. After all, God did identify himself with his people
in Jesus of Nazareth, coming to them in the same weakness and frailty
and vulnerability of human nature at Bethlehem *before* he spoke to
them the Word of judgment and hope. How much more, then, will
preachers in all their frailty and vulnerability identify themselves with
their people and make it crystal clear that the prophetic Word is
addressed to themselves as well as to others in the community of
believers. The use of pronouns in the sermon will provide a clue.
Prophetic judgment is never addressed to "you" but to "us." "We"
are under the judgment of God. "You and I" live under God's judgment, rather than the community of believers living under the judgment of the preacher. (See the further discussion of prophetic
preaching in chapter 6 below.) Isaiah 6 provides the biblical basis for
prophetic preaching: "I am a man of unclean lips, and I dwell in the
midst of a people of unclean lips; for my eyes have seen the King, the
Lord of hosts" (Isa. 6:5).

So we return to the image of the preacher, Bible in uplifted hand, as
the image of the preacher's authority—so long as we recall that there
are three stories implicit in that image: (1) The biblical story, apart
from which there would be no preaching; (2) the preacher's own
individual story, through which the biblical story is filtered and which
adds the preacher's own individual witness that the biblical story has
in fact become the preacher's story; (3) the story of the listeners, the
community of believers, who have provided the place and occasion for
preaching and who have called the preacher to do on their behalf what
the preacher has been trained by them to do—so to interpret the biblical story that light is shed on all three stories.

It is readily recognized that this kind of authority is not sufficiently
clear-cut or authoritarian for some in the church—or out of the
church—today. In a period of frighteningly rapid change and of future
shock, there is an understandable itch on the part of many for dog-

matic, authoritarian, oversimplified answers to questions for which we are not given those kinds of answers. So Robert E. C. Browne adds a cautionary word: "What ministers of the Word say may seem too little to live on, but they must not go beyond their authority in a mistaken attempt to make their authority strong and clear. That going beyond is always the outcome of an atheistic anxiety, or a sign that the man of God has succumbed to speak as a god, to come in his own name and to be his own authority."[2]

NOTES

1. Karl Barth, *The Preaching of the Gospel* (Philadelphia: Westminster Press, 1963), p. 9.

2. Robert E. C. Browne, *The Ministry of the Word* (Philadelphia: Fortress Press, 1976), p. 40. Browne's is a seminal and rewarding book on preaching, and the chapter on authority is well worth pondering.

SERMON:

The View from Mount Nebo

Joseph Sittler

NOTE: One is sometimes called upon so to preach as to correct an imbalance, violently to attack an understanding of the Christian faith which, if not corrected, permits people to reject an authentic Christian faith because they reject a caricature.

The following sermon was preached to such a situation. A summer camp under presumably Christian auspices was manned by several hundred students, and they assembled each Sunday for an hour of worship. The prevailing ethos of the camp was Christian—experiential, sentimental. Personal testimonies around an emotion-stirring campfire were a regular evening feature.

For many students this procedure was normal, authentic, an accustomed way. For others it was abnormal, inauthentic, strange. But the students who rejected the custom felt that they were somehow outside the orbit of normal Christian experience. And the feeling troubled them. This sermon was addressed to the outsiders.

And Moses went up from the plains of Moab to Mount Nebo, to the top of Pisgah, which is opposite Jericho. And the Lord showed him all the land, Gilead as far as Dan, all Naphtali, the land of Ephraim and Manasseh, all the land of Judah as far as the Western Sea, the Negeb, and the Plain, that is, the valley of Jericho the city of palm trees, as far as Zoar. And the Lord said to him, "This is the land of which I swore to Abraham, to Isaac, and to Jacob, 'I will give it to your descendants.' I have let you see it with your eyes, but you shall not go over there." So Moses the servant of the Lord died there in the land of

[Joseph Sittler, *The Care of the Earth and Other University Sermons* (Philadelphia: Fortress Press, 1964).]

Moab, according to the word of the Lord, and he buried him in the valley in the land of Moab opposite Bethpeor; but no man knows the place of his burial to this day. Moses was a hundred and twenty years old when he died; his eye was not dim, nor his natural force abated. And the people of Israel wept for Moses in the plains of Moab thirty days; then the days of weeping and mourning for Moses were ended.

And Joshua the son of Nun was full of the spirit of wisdom, for Moses had laid his hands upon him; so the people of Israel obeyed him, and did as the Lord had commanded Moses. And there has not arisen a prophet since in Israel like Moses, whom the Lord knew face to face, none like him for all the signs and the wonders which the Lord sent him to do in the land of Egypt, to Pharaoh and to all his servants and to all his land, and for all the mighty power and all the great and terrible deeds which Moses wrought in the sight of all Israel.

Deuteronomy 34

One should not oversimplify the Christian doctrine of the Holy Spirit. That doctrine declares that faith is a work of God's Spirit, that it is God alone who can cause a man in full personal decision to make the Christian confession.

But sometimes we so speak, or more often sing, of the work of the Holy Spirit as to reduce to a single and simple way the enormous variety of ways the Holy Spirit accomplishes his work. One such over-simplification is celebrated in the hymn that has a melancholy popularity among many young peoples' groups.

> Blessed assurance, Jesus is mine.
> Oh, what a foretaste of glory divine.

What this hymn suggests is that nothing Christian is authentic until and unless it has become a blessed assurance in some specifiable, warm, pervasive, and crucial experience.

This assumption points to a truth, and it encourages an error. The truth is that man is an organic whole, integral, and that there is a continuity between outside and inside, appearance and reality. There is a momentum between confession and total being. But the error is the assumption that Christian faith is normally identical with what has been confirmed in that way. That assumption is not only erroneous, it is dangerous; for it invites the mind to reduce the Christian pronouncement and claim to those elements which have been certified in the heat of one's individual experience. Such an error is both reductive and perverting, for it shrinks and twists the magnificence, the scope, and the objectivity of Christian fact to the dimension of personal and largely temperamental endowments. It tempts us to hang the reality of God, the compass of his demands, the scope of biblical and theological meaning upon a febrile nail: the warmth and immediacy of a feeling of blessed assurance.

This subjectivizing of the Christian faith presents problems for us. Instead of speaking of these abstractly I have chosen to speak of one such problem as I know it concretely. For some years I was dean of students in a theological seminary of my church and had frequently to talk with students who came to me disturbed because their sense of vocation was not as strong, or as inwardly certified, as they felt it ought to be if they were going to be ordained ministers of the Christian gospel. They said, "I believe the gospel and that a man ought to preach it. But how do I know that this task is for me? I don't have that interior confirmation whereby I can have a sense of absolute certainty in my vocation as a Christian minister."

I have sometimes been able to be of help to such students because I have walked and walk that same rope. I feel the same absence of this "blessed assurance" in my own life. I too make uncertified postulation of the Christian faith, uncertified, that is, by auxiliary feelings that are supposed somehow to make it more true. In my experience in teaching and preaching the story of the Christian faith I recall an instance in my own parish when I was preaching straight through Philippians. I did pretty well through the first part of the first chapter. This part is historical and reportorial; I could simply say that this is what happened to Paul, and this is the way he responded. Then I came to the verse that really separates the men from the boys: verse 21 in the first chapter, "For to me to live is Christ, and to die is gain." I had to begin my sermon by saying, "I must declare to you something this morning that I do not know anything about." My job was not to say, "This is true, and I can testify that it is true," because I would have been a liar to say that. I had not yet come to the point (and I have not yet come to it, either) where I can say, "If I die today it is all right with me. For me to die is gain." I do not have the gifts of grace whereby I can say this. My duty instead is to say that the man who said the other true things in the first chapter of Philippians did not suddenly turn into a phony when he said this! "I don't know that this is so, but Saint Paul knew that it was so" was a proper statement. My duty was to say that grace has this magnificent possibility, it *can* do that to a man, and for Paul, it did. He could then say that "if they take me to Rome and cut my head off next week or whether I return to you at Philippi is no longer the fundamental issue."

I wish I had so rich and gallant a gift. But my duty is not to reduce the message to the size of what I have or have not; it is proper sometimes to declare what one does not know.

But is this just my problem? Is it just my pilgrimage? I think not. There are thousands of students today to whom the Christian faith must be declared as if they too stood in that same position. And it is for that reason that I have chosen the title "The View from Mount Nebo." It suggests different perspectives for looking in upon things. There are many mountains in the Bible: Mount Hermon, Mount Zion, Mount Calvary. But there is that other peak, Mount Nebo. And I ask you to regard this peak as a kind of symbol by which to elucidate a way of standing within the problem of "blessed assurance."

Think of three perspectives from which one can envision and begin to talk about the Christian faith. First, the perspective from within. Most talk about Christianity does, and should, proceed from this warm, immediate perspective from within the body of the people of God in Christ. They speak out of and in the language of this beloved community which knows what it means to have been redeemed from the insecurities and egocentricities of perilous life. They are firmly held by the action of God, speak of it with adoration, understanding, enthusiasm. The great objective Story of Christianity has been reenacted within their own experience in such a way that an outer nativity at Bethlehem has become an inner nativity whereby they know a new birth. An incarnation *there* has wrought a strange new man *here*. A death in the great Story is now interpreted to be a death of self from which one rises in answer to the outer resurrection to a newness of life in every moment of his breathing existence. This perspective from within, which I see and partly understand, is always the first central perspective for declaring the Christian Story. Christ is love, and joy, peace, hope; and all these gifts are given by the Holy Ghost. They are, as Paul says, "the fruits of the Spirit."

As your preacher this morning, it is only honest to say that I have never known fully that kind of life within the full, warm power of that faith for whose declaration I am an ordained minister. The very term *Christian experience,* as generally understood, has small meaning for me. I have not seen any burning bushes. I have not pounded at the door of God's grace with the passion of a Martin Luther. John Wesley's "strangely warmed" heart at Aldersgate Street—this is not my street. I have not the possibility to say of the Christian faith what many honest men have said about it. But I have come to see that to declare as a gift of God what I do not fully possess is, nevertheless, a duty of obedience. Is the opulence of the grace of God to be measured by my inventory? Is the great catholic faith of nineteen centuries to be reduced to my interior dimensions? Are the arching lines of the gracious possible to be pulled down to the little spurts of my personal compass? Is the great heart of the reality of God to speak in only the broken accent that I can follow after? No. That ought not to be. Therefore, one is proper and right when he sometimes talks of things he doesn't know all about. In obedience to the bigness of the story which transcends his own apprehension, one may do this.

 A second perspective is the perspective from without. The first perspective is characterized by participation, the second by detachment. The view from without has not the same legitimacy or the same kind of power as the view from within. But it has, nevertheless, its own power, its own function, and it addresses students of today with a particular kind of velocity. It is primarily critical, reportorial, or as the student in sciences would call it, phenomenological. It asks what it means to be a Christian. What does this community called Christian intend, whence did it come, what did it affirm as it came into history, how is this community constituted, what does it declare about the nature of truth and reality, how has it embodied its affirmations in cultural-historical institutions and in ethics?

Now that is perhaps not a very exciting way to be a Christian. But I should like to suggest that you think of what the Christian community owes to the quiet men who view from this second perspective. These are men who never raise their voices in declaration or declamation, seldom praise in public, never offer moving testimonials. Who knows what goes on in the hearts of men who lack the grace of adoration, of passion, of immediate blessed assurance, who lack full knowledge of God, who must live out their lives in hard, dutiful obedience to lesser, cooler graces because their lives are unattended by the hotter ones? These men's Christian lives are given, rather, to discernment, critical work, the effort to achieve a precise description of what is really involved in becoming and being a Christian.

I once studied for some months in a German university. One of my professors was a great teacher of preaching. This man could not preach, and he never tried to. He was too honest to claim to have what the Bible talks about and promises. But he knew what the biblical promise was, he knew that when the Bible talks of the kingdom of God it does not mean habitual piety, puritan mores, better homes and gardens, middle-class respectability, soul sweetness and body cleanliness, inoffensive community acceptability. He knew that when he was talking about redemption, salvation, sin, faith, grace he was talking about huge and clear realities. He would not permit us to palm off phony realities in the name of these. He knew that whether he had the gift of these realities or not, they do constitute what it means to be a Christian.

The third perspective is that of many of us who are students. It has a peculiar pathos, a peculiar toughness, honesty, and promise for the days that lie ahead. It is the perspective of many today who do not know if they ought to call themselves Christians at all but who are saddened in their feeling of being outside the Christian company.

It is this third perspective which is suggested by our lesson from Deuteronomy. Will you recall the Scripture lesson from Deuteronomy which talks about Moses on Mount Nebo in the land of Moab. Recall what you know about Moses. This man was a strong, spiritual, and faithful man.

He was a strong man. He steadfastly pointed with all the force of his massive personal power to the will of God for his people. He kept their ears open to God, he kept their faces turned toward their destiny, and he kicked their reluctant feet along the road to their heavenly possession. Michelangelo's great actualization of the figure of Moses is not wrong: that awesome figure is all the trouble and the Exodus and the hard wilderness of Israel portrayed in stone.

Moses was a spiritual man. He was determined by the Spirit that called him to live his life under a certain discipline and task. Spiritual does not mean to be wrapped in a kind of holy gas which becomes ignited around testimonial campfires. For Moses it meant to have his will and decisions determined by the Spirit of God. He knew that God had a will for his people and that man's spirit was to be subjected to that great Spirit. He was therefore a lawgiver, that is, the voice of the Spirit of God who constituted this particular people and gave them particular laws. Moses would never let them forget that—and Deuteronomy is his monument.

Moses was a faithful man. He obeyed even when he did not understand. He held to the command. He obeyed the vision in Egypt, in the wilderness, on Mount Sinai, and even on Mount Nebo. There is where we see him in this lesson.

Moses on Mount Nebo is a man in the situation of many of us who feel we must confess and serve a faith whose gifts to us are not given with all the opulence we might desire, and in whose lives the very gifts of grace do not control us who are the declarers of these same gifts. Here is a perspective from which many a man must view the life of the church, the tradition, and the pathos of his own position. Moses saw clearly, but he could not enter into what he saw. The poorest child of that people who entered into the land of promise had what Moses, who led them to the land, could never have. Moses had sight without actuality; he had knowledge without possession. Moses knew more about what Israel meant than most men in Israel. But he died outside the land.

At this particular moment in our religion and intellectual history the perspective from Mount Nebo is a necessary one. It is good for many of today's college students to see the man who from Nebo's peak was yet strong, spiritual, faithful. For students are being invited to sit in the cozy rooms of religious togetherness and seek violently after "commitment"—a kind of contemporary term for the older blessed assurance. And many of them can't bring it off. The conventional standard psychological equipment of blessed assurance has not been given them. They are critical, historically self-conscious, they know a thing or two about the vast variety of stages on the way to the Christian confession, and they are not disposed to indulge in these too-quick oversimplifications which university studies have warned them against.

It is at such a moment that the perspective from Mount Nebo may be useful to us. The men of Mount Nebo are the obedient children of both participation and detachment. They know and they do not know fully. They participate because they come from the tradition and tuition of the faith, and have been so deeply formed by it that they cannot escape its terms, its claims, its ethics. And they do not want to. They know the power and the good of the God relationship in all things: they know it to be true, and rich, and free. They want to be open to the renewing power of the Holy, but at the same time, while they participate, they do not fully enter. Their participation is a kind of "hurt" participation: they do not possess those gifts of the Spirit—love, joy, peace, hope—which would permit them without a kind of sardonic footnote to sing, "Blessed assurance, Jesus is mine." Nevertheless, they want to affirm those very gifts as being a possibility of God for the world.

Now from the inside, for many of us tormented by this precise perspective, this means that we must sometimes envision with the mind what the heart cannot yet confirm, must see and affirm with clear intellectual sight what we have not been given the grace to celebrate in actual life. And yet, how great is our debt to the men *without* grace who out of the passion of their poverty sing the songs of grace!

Think for instance of Sören Kierkegaard, that great Christian man, who out of a loveless love has written of love with excruciating penetration. Just as the hungry talk of food, or the thirsty of water, so does this mordant man who loved hopelessly write of human love with a penetration and a passion which few men have ever equaled. Here is a strange fact: precision in knowledge and statement may have two mothers, and they are in contradiction. There is a precision which is born of knowledge: the clear, joyous precision of the insider who lives completely with the faith. St. Francis had it. John Calvin had it. And there is the other precision: the precision begotten of deprivation, the tormented precision of vision without gift. There are men in the Christian tradition who have described the reality of certain graces because they lived their lives not within the vitality and fragrance of these graces, but because they stood outside longingly looking in and described with tormented precision what they saw. They are the men of Mount Nebo who see what their feet cannot touch and out of negation forge those clear descriptions which then become the dear possession of the children of the land. These are the men who in sheer thought forge ideas in longing that other men affirm in quiet and unquestioning possession. Pathos gives a toughness that affirmation profits by.

Now, you will tell me, faith without works is dead, and you are quite right. The men of Mount Nebo know this with an excruciating clarity that the calm quoters of the passage seldom know. And out of their poverty they fashion the only possible gift they can bring to the faith—a clarity given to the bereft that enables others to know and to find.

On the peak of Nebo, between participation without substance and detachment without peace, they add their astringent voice to the song of faith. Without the lean men of Nebo the people on Mount Zion are always tempted to become fat. There is a beatitude in the New Testament which reads, "Blessed are they that hunger and thirst, . . . for they shall be filled." I would suggest to this disconsolate student generation that in the long history of the intellectual life of the church, and having a poignant force in these confusing days when the very nature of Christian truth and its relation to the world is being refashioned, a second little beatitude may be wrought out for our comfort in a lesser and a stranger way: "Blessed also are they that continue to hunger and thirst without being filled." For just to hunger and thirst and to know without settling for it that you *do* hunger and thirst is given a kind of negative benediction. Hunger, unabated, is a kind of testimony to the reality of food. To want to have may become a strange kind of having.

PART TWO

THE LISTENERS

3

The Story of Our Times

Charles L. Rice

A community tells its story—to itself—as culture. This significant storytelling takes diverse and unpredictable forms: urban planning, the arts, cooking, advertising, architecture, religious observance, dress, patterns of work, and forms of leisure. The ways in which people use surplus time and energy are especially revealing of their values. What would some archaeologist of the twenty-fifth century make of us as she or he sifted our dumps and unearthed, in almost any town,

> . . . an asphalt road
> And a thousand lost golf balls?[1]

Automobile fenders, neon, Sunday afternoon sports, fast food—these, no less than the evening news or music, are the media of culture. Every cultural phenomenon, from the Broadway stage to the main-street facades of a country town, can be read with an eye to the real concerns and hopes of a people.

Is there, then, a common story that we can assume? Is the earth, a small blue ball floating in space, the home of a common humanity? Or in a closer range, do we who share a common citizenship live in a matrix of shared values? Or must we narrow our sights even further? To black culture, WASP culture, Catholic, gay?

In any group of people, however narrow or broad their horizons, commonly held images are probably as important as strictly personal experiences. There is such a thing as corporate autobiography.[2] We would probably be able to hear more clearly both the story of our times and the gospel if we were more like the people of Israel, who, whatever internal or external crisis they faced, were called to remember what Yahweh had done for them as a people and to repent and turn toward their destiny as a chosen nation. They had a well-defined and often-rehearsed common story. And someone speaking on its wavelength could convey to them almost any message.

But do *we* have a common story? If Jesus told his parables today, to what common consciousness would he speak, and in what shared experience would he find his material?

Dean Hoge says that most of us live by values which express themselves in powerful social realities: family, career, standard of living, and health (where that is a factor not to be taken for granted).[3] Hoge believes that behind all ideological loyalties, religious confessions, public orations, and national creeds, this hierarchy, which can be understood as a creed and given creedal form, is what actually determines our economic, political, and religious behavior. Politicians are elected, leaders rewarded, denominations adhered to, and social and ethnic groups variously tolerated, exploited, or scapegoated according to their serviceability in terms of this tacit creed. Among church members there is a fairly easy identification of Christ with these values, a fact which is apparent across a spectrum so wide as to include both a demanding and doctrinaire Mormonism and the popular optimism of much electronic religion.

If this analysis is true of church people, it is true also of the public at large, where such a "creed" enjoys a similar favor. A close analysis of the media, for example, will corroborate Hoge on this point: it is precisely the archetypal realities of the human condition—love, sex, money, death—which appear as the stock-in-trade of popular entertainment, journalism, and advertising. The soap opera, to take the most obvious example, weds the drama of love, sex, money, and death to advertising, and the total experience seems to be cathartic for a large number of afternoon viewers. The media concentrate on those archetypal realities in which our aspirations and anxieties, both individual and social, are focused. What hopes and fears, of each and all, are touched by an advertisement for perfume or deodorant, or by a story—however perverse—of a disintegrating family, middle-aged Casanova, or wayward daughter?

Consider on another level, as an example, the anxiety which centers on the nuclear family, one of the archetypal realities. The anxiety is so pronounced that while few will advocate, many can be heard to predict its imminent demise. And because the family is seen as foundational, it becomes a focus for an otherwise more generalized anxiety about the pluralization of society, the breakdown of familiar structures, and changing sexual attitudes and practices. Thus divorced persons and homosexuals are regarded as threats to the *family* and therefore to the society: recent crusades against civil rights for homosexuals have marched under a banner which read, "Save Our Children!" Likewise, despite the removal of many legal and economic sanctions against the divorced, separation from one's spouse is still seen as socially undesirable; it threatens those whose marriages while still "whole" are increasingly uncomfortable—and is therefore seen as a threat to the entire culture.

The irrational disdain for both of these groups in large measure simply reflects the overload of sexual and social anxiety which attaches to the family as the paradigmatic model of the idealized and stable past. There is apparently a deep need in our culture to center social order and meaning in the nostalgically perceived past, that is, the nuclear family, and to confine love and sex to the manageable and familiar dimensions of the traditional family structure. It is therefore no surprise that this need grows more acute as the culture becomes ever more dependent upon the exploitation of sexuality for the selling of goods and services and for the stimulation of the imagination. So it is that in California nude beaches, frequented by families as well as by others, fall under a ban, while prurient sex titillates the whole society on newsstands, television, and the movie screens. In most quarters, loyalty to the idealized (if not the actual) family is tantamount to loyalty to God, church, and country.

What is true of the family is true also of career and standard of living, which for most people are inseparable and which are both in turn closely tied to sex and family. Who can doubt that Marx was at least partially right in his estimate of the place of economic motivation in human action? Can the resistance to equal opportunity and compensation for women be explained without reference to sexual anxiety: What is it to be a man if not to make more money and to be in charge? What is it to be a woman if not to be related to such a man? Philip Slater illumines those questions in a book which is very helpful for the preacher and deserves our close attention.[4] For our present purposes, however, we simply raise the question, Are we sufficiently aware, those of us who preach, of the resilient cultural foundation which underlies and shapes the structures in which our people live and within which we inevitably preach? How can the preacher's voice be heard, and can it make any difference, among the many subtle voices which begin to speak at the mere mention of job, house, or women? Those "creedal" foundations are not easily shaken.

So W. D. Davies, the New Testament scholar, asked for his estimate of the effectiveness of the pulpit today, replied: "Preaching is like church bells. It is a familiar sound which is welcome so long as it doesn't wake us from sleep or interrupt some important activity." If we take that for what it is—a half-truth—and if we credit Hoge's analysis, then it is clear that preaching will be accepted by listeners so long as it conforms with their basic view of the world in terms of family, career, and standard of living. When it does not fit that grid, it will more likely be tolerated as "just preaching" or rejected outright as being irrelevant.

Is it not true that we know at some deep level the story by which people, including ourselves, are living—and the near impossibility of shaking any of those foundations? How else can we explain the relative silence or ineffectiveness of the pulpit on the pressing issues of the day, all of which threaten family, career, and standard of living?—the modification of personal and national life-style toward less consumption; the rethinking of human sexuality; the struggle of women and ethnic groups for economic and social equality; the application of science and technology to genetics and medicine; armaments; aging and death. None of these problems and none of the movements which they are spawning has any recognizable place in the story by which most of our people live, a well-known if not clearly articulated way of life with which both the average North American and the church as an institution have identified themselves. How, then, can biblical preaching be heard, and culture transformed by the gospel? This question is addressed in a direct and powerful way by "The Two Battles," a sermon by Frederick Buechner which follows the next chapter.

Buechner distinguishes clearly between the common human struggle for survival and success on the one hand, and on the other the struggle whose terms are those of the gospel and whose consummation is the kingdom of God. What is important for preachers, in distinguishing one battle from the other, is to see that there are stresses within the culture itself which may become the openings through which the gospel can enter and transform our common life. The story of our times is not altogether cohesive, and it is at the points where "things fall apart and the center cannot hold" that we wait for the advent of the Word of God.[5]

Perhaps only a preacher ("Friends, we are living in a time . . .") or the author of one of those "Inside . . ." books, written after two weeks inside Russia or India, would attempt these next few pages. Who, living in these very days, could write what it is to live toward the end of the twentieth century? And if one could do so, the picture would have changed before anyone could read what had been written. For part of the story of our times is exactly that there is too much of that story; there is today an overstimulation that prevents us from assimilating our experience. We might do better to take a cue from Steinbeck, Kuralt, or Moyers, who, when they wanted to hear America's story, took to the *road*. Or we might go to see the best plays or take time to read some novels that could tell us our story. Nevertheless . . .

John Crossan has said that paradox is to language as eschaton is to world: the straining of language and history point beyond themselves.[6] In the paradoxes and stresses of our common story, and in the cracks and gaps which are opening in our creed regarding our foundational realities as they respond to the shocks and stresses of the story we are living, we may learn more about the present-but-coming kingdom and find language in which to witness to the hope of the kingdom. Since the perceptive preacher must deal with these polarities, it may be helpful to mention a number of them here.

One set of cracks is visible in the experience of personality-in-community. Eliot has said it well:

> What life have you if you have not life together?
> There is no life that is not in community,
> And no community not lived in praise of GOD.
> Even the anchorite who meditates alone,
> For whom the days and nights repeat the praise of GOD,
> Prays for the Church, the Body of Christ incarnate.

And now you live dispersed on ribbon roads,
And no man knows or cares who is his neighbour
Unless his neighbour makes too much disturbance,
But all dash to and fro in motor cars,
Familiar with the roads and settled nowhere.
But every son would have his motor cycle,
And daughters ride away on casual pillions.
. . . .
When the Stranger says: "What is the meaning of this city?
Do you huddle close together because you love each other?"
What will you answer? "We all dwell together
To make money from each other"? or "This is a community"?
And the Stranger will depart and return to the desert.
O my soul, be prepared for the coming of the stranger,
Be prepared for him who knows how to ask questions.[7]

Our history and geography have made us individualists, but the realities of our life together conflict with that overriding characteristic. Urbanization, rapid communication and transportation, the politicizing of issues which impinge upon the personal and private —all exacerbate the unresolved conflict between the individual and society. It is increasingly hard for us on the one hand to live privately, and on the other hand it is equally difficult for society to hold together as an aggregate of individualists. Privacy and individuality are essential to the health of the community, but privatism and individualism are inimical to it.

We seem to be at a loss for a tradition—a spiritual way, a national ethos, or a civil religion—which is capable of moving beyond the equally unsatisfactory positions of conventionalism and permissivism. Consequently the society is prone to hypocrisy, and individuals are torn between moralism and license—and that is comical, or deeply tragic, or perhaps both at once. And from a theological perspective we must ask whether our society will ever be able to become a community unless we develop a deepened sense of the comic and the tragic in human life. Without a sense of comedy we are unable to look at ourselves as we are, upright mammals with egg on our faces, sharing the common experience of being human. Comedy allows us to laugh at that, and the bias of comedy is toward faith. The tragic vision also sees unblinkingly the human condition. One, or both perhaps, will be essential to the development and survival of true human community.

And in theological perspective, the comic sense and the tragic vision are the preparation for the grace of God, which is the source and ground of both responsible individuality and free community.

Do we as people still have any chance to achieve true community? In the case of the United States, the answer may not be as clear as it once was, for it is no longer the nation it once was. It has devastated another nation, and lost a war, in Vietnam. And unless its people find a way to face up to themselves as a people, it may never find its way to a responsible and gracious society. The question, then, is whether that people will be found still to have the resources to enter into the tragic vision or to take a comic view of their common life. If they can find the resources for neither, hopes for true community are dim indeed. For we can hardly be satisfied with the present alternatives: a nostalgic conservatism holding out for a pristine way of life that never was; a possibility theology which turns away from the dark side of life and ignores the central image of the Christian faith, the cross; and a spate of egocentric movements which have turned a method into an ideology, so that everything is pronounced OK in the same way as one would express approval of bites taken only from the shiny side of an apple. Only a very affluent and constantly entertained society can survive for long on such placebos. What we are looking for is a way to face the world as it is and each other as we are and still be able to give and receive freedom. We want, in short, to be together, but not merely on the ground of respectability, illusion, or downright hypocrisy.

There is an intimation of the possibility for a community of a new kind in *The Changing Room*, a play by David Storey.[8] This is a play about twenty-two men brought together every Saturday to play rugby. They are coal miners and factory workers—there is one schoolteacher —in an English industrial town. This particular Saturday is bitterly cold, but the locker room where they suit up is warm, if not with plenty of coal, with banter and getting themselves up for the game. One of them is a big guy, almost seven feet tall, who has a new tool kit. He is like a child on Christmas Day, showing it to his teammates, and as they strip down they all become more like children at play than competitors, suddenly oblivious to the world they have taken off with their street clothes. They go out to play, looking and sounding like so many overgrown boys in short white pants and striped shirts, and they come in at the half, bloodied and half frozen, covered with mud, patting and reassuring the big guy who has a bloody nose. They rally and talk it up and go trotting back for more of the same.

The last act, after the game is over, shows all of them in a common bath, one big tub, singing obscene songs, water fighting and snapping towels, dancing and flaunting their nudity outrageously, completely vulnerable. We forget whether they have won or lost the game; what is happening now, as they wash the mud and blood from each other, is what it is all about.

In the last scene, after they have all put on their clothes and gone out one by one, the custodian comes in. He moves about slowly, gathering up their woebegone shirts and shorts and wet towels, carrying them over both arms with the reverence of a sexton putting away vestments after Communion.

The preacher who would address in the present day a people whose concepts and experiences of individuality and community are as threatened and confused as Eliot suggests would do well to ponder long and deeply such stories as *The Changing Room,* for it is in just such a manner that the intimations of new ways and of a new age can move into the interstices of our experience and awareness of a society which seems otherwise so perverse, so sterile, and so moribund.

Our culture is baffled about individuality and community, and it is anxious about its bafflement. It is anxious also about another pair of tendencies or values: pluralism and provincialism.

We can only imagine the diversity of the eighty-five million people who first watched "Roots" on television, but one thing is sure: most of them are the grandchildren, however far removed, of immigrants. They know at one level or another the tension between mass culture and the identity of a person or a region. Is Harvey Cox correct in his assertion that the more pluralistic and complex our society becomes, the more we will need to recover and celebrate our distinctive stories?[9] Josiah Royce would have thought so. He predicted that mass communication and standardized modes of living would reduce society to a "harassed dead level of mediocrity." And he didn't have television!

Royce opposed the melting pot as a social ideal. Instead, he said, we should actively cultivate provincialism, the appreciation of one's own background, locale, and customs. Loyalty to the larger community, even "loyalty to loyalty," would be learned in the primary group, and the larger society could expect to be held together and to flourish only as people valued their personal and ethnic provinces.

Although Royce's ideas have already exercised a pronounced effect upon H. Richard Niebuhr, they may yet come more fully into their own. For the more complex and personalized our social and economic environment becomes, and the more pluralistic our society, the greater will be our interest in local color, oral history, biography, regional customs, ethnic folkways, and even denominations. In an overwhelmingly pluralistic society, is it not the sense of one's own time and place which leads to a new valuing of the identity and worth of other persons, and even of their privacy and property?

Jack Burden is a young man of the new South, and he is on the make. His past is a dim blur, and he is not sure that he wants to find out about it. He is on his way to the top. In one scene, he has just had a talk with his mother, who worries about Jack and wants him to get married and settle down:

> I went upstairs and lay in the bathtub with the hot water up to my ears and knew that it was over. It was over again. I would get in my car, right after dinner, and drive like hell toward town over the new concrete slab between the black, mist-streaked fields, and get to town about midnight and go up to my hotel room where nothing was mine and nothing knew my name and nothing had a thing to say about anything that had ever happened.

Later, after learning how he was born illegitimate, and who his father is, Jack expresses his feeling of new liberation:

> If you could not accept the past and its burden there was no future, for without one there cannot be the other, and . . . if you could accept the past you might hope for the future, for only out of the past can you make the future.[10]

In the Italian movie *The Conformist* a young man sits up in bed on a fine morning. Fully dressed in suit, tie, hat, and shiny shoes, he announces, "I have decided to conform." Before the movie ends he has joined the Fascists, betrayed his friends, and committed murder. As the city falls we see him alone, wandering the bombed-out streets, and then in one small episode of unguarded passion, we see a man who in denying who he is and in tyrannizing himself has become a nobody, the mere tool of tyrants.

How does the preacher enable listeners to understand who they are as unique persons and where they have come from, and to affirm and celebrate their unique selves—without allowing them to become mere egotists?

There is now a third polarity with which our culture will force the perceptive preacher to deal. It is the polarity of power and limits. One is reminded that life in our society is in general heroic. The jet plane and automobile give most of us a way around the limitations of animal locomotion, and the shopping center provides ready escape from the ordinary: there is the illusion of transcending time and mortality.[11] When things go wrong, or when winter (or just boredom) sets in, people are likely to get out the credit card or buy a ticket. The limitations of the human condition seem to be overcome, and even the reality of death to be set aside. "The Prayer of the Cock" captures perfectly the unreality of the mood: "I am your servant, only . . . do not forget, Lord, I make the sun rise."[12]

Alongside these heroic impulses, in paradoxical tension, is an abiding love of simplicity, home, our town, and a deep-seated realism. We are almost relieved when a snowstorm or gas shortage immobilizes our cars and reduces the arena of our activity to the limits of our legs and imaginations. At home, shut in, and playing simple games or making bread, we become aware of the joy and health of living within human limits, and of the cost to our psyches of our "normal" patterns of living in affluent mobility.

The stresses which will mount if we become more and more affluent and mobile will intensify the question, What is it to be human? What are our real possibilities? We are in need of a theology which can speak to both our limits and our possibilities, that could move us beyond compensation and entertainment to wholeness and joy.

The Gin Game is a play about two people whose lives have been pruned down, by time and circumstance, to a card table and each other, and about their dogged efforts to make something of what they have left.[13] The limits of their lives are easy to see. Her children now live far away; he has lost what money he may have made, and home for both of them is a formerly grand house with elderly tenants to match its peeling portico and sagging, leaky porch. The two of them spend their time out there—for them it is a breezy veranda—playing gin, at least trying to play gin.

The trouble is that for some uncanny reason she, the novice, wins every game, and he has a quick temper. As he deals out the cards for yet another go, the television set flickers through the French doors, and occasionally a church choir sings in the dim inner recesses of what must have been the dining room. But they allow no distractions. Raging and crying, he starting each game cocky, she learning to swear, with sedated people in the house and a storm booming outside, they try—across the shaky little table which becomes the very universe—to communicate with each other.

What kinds of power do people want? What kinds do they need? What are the limits under which they chafe and fret? Which are real? Which necessary, which inevitable, which imaginary? Which culturally imposed?

There is a fourth major question lodged against some of the easy assumptions on which our societal creed of life is based. It is that increasingly urgent question which is posed by the gradual depletion—and by the unequal distribution—of the earth's resources. Hear Adam Finnerty: "This ocean liner . . . is in danger of sinking . . . not so much because of the hordes of hungry passengers clinging to the rail and massed together in its dirty and dangerous holds as because of the deportment of the first-class passengers."[14] Even if we seem unbounded in our possibilities, the earth has limits: air, water, energy, arable land, plants and animals of the sustaining ecosystem—none can be taken for granted any longer. Economics, understood as the growth of the gross national product, has dominated our attitudes toward the environment. Now in consequence mother earth is beginning to show the marks of her abuse, and judgment appears as shortage, the most acute form of which is hunger widespread across the world.

What is the good life? Marianne Micks has said that the cycles by which we actually live are oriented not to Advent and Easter but to weekends and vacations.[15] We can endure a life which is not so good if on weekends and vacations we can get away to real, rich life. Affluent, mobile leisure is good for the economy, generally hard on the environment, and a point of stress at which very human questions become obviously theological: What is it to live well on the earth? Is the good life the maximum consumption possible, or is it minimal? Or something else?

Our most immediate environment is of course our bodies. The impact of economic motivation on our life in the flesh is enormous. We are only beginning to realize that wholesome natural food, a clean and peaceful environment, and a balance of work and play are essential to well-being. As for medicine, we are floundering before the impact of economics and technology on the care and disposition of the human body, and we are just approaching new frontiers of natural and spiritual healing. An opening appears, then, precisely at these points where faced with new data and new technology we are being forced to decide all over again what the good life is.

Kurt Vonnegut's novel *Cat's Cradle* ends in the ultimate ecological disaster. Ice-nine, developed for the Pentagon by an American research scientist to keep the Marines out of the mud, has a melting point above a hundred degrees Fahrenheit. The problem is that the process of freezing cannot be reversed, and at the end of the story the whole earth is locked in apocalyptic frost.

Much of the action takes place on the island of San Lorenzo, a place of cynical politics, an extreme disparity of poverty and wealth, and most important, the religion of Bokononism. Officially outlawed but practiced by virtually the whole populace, Bokononism has only one ritual, *boko-maru,* which is practiced in secret; two people sit on the floor facing each other, the soles of their bare feet pressed together, perhaps singing Bokonon's "Calypso":

> We will touch our feet, yes,
> Yes, for all we're worth,
> And we will love each other, yes,
> Yes, like we love our Mother Earth.[16]

The movie *Close Encounters* came as a surprise, to say the least. We expected a cinematic space thriller to be terrifying, and the strange visitors to be green and menacing. But when the little people come down the ramp of their astounding ship they are modeled on human fetuses, childlike in their intelligence, simplicity, and eagerness to communicate. The film reaches out into space to find nonhumans more human than the humans we know!

What *is* the good life for which we hunger?

Let us consider yet one more polarity which suggests an opening in the creedal compactness of our culture, an opening for the gospel of God. This polarity is that of poetry and positivism. "It is not objective proof of God's existence that we want but, whether we use religious language for it or not, the experience of God's presence."[17]

In the fifties and sixties a certain kind of religious article appeared as regularly as the *Reader's Digest.* A scientist would write on "Sixteen Reasons Why I Believe in God," and the reader would give a great sigh of relief that the scientists still had a place for faith in their scheme of things. Those articles, for all their religiosity, functioned, however, only as one more form of positivism, the reduction of human experience to conform to limited interests or perspectives.

Let us look more closely. The positivist is one who wants to make things fit, and whatever movement or ideology is *the* way to truth at the moment becomes the box into which everything is forced to fit. Virtually any world view can lead to its positivistic form: philosophical schools, fundamentalism, pragmatism, moralism, political systems. In the "Why I Believe in God" articles, what the scientist says, whatever its own merits may be, counts, not least, because science has been technologically successful. Who in our culture, having received all we have at the hands of science and hoping for more, would doubt the testimony of a scientist? The scientist's confession of faith could well be both earnest and well informed. But the decision to print it, knowing it will be widely and well received, is mute but powerful testimony to scientism, to the comprehensive triumph of the technological, rather than to God.

The scene is shifting, though. Science itself makes place for a more modest, even reverent approach to nature, and pragmatists are called to take account of the good, the true, and the beautiful. For superb examples of the poetic reverence of a scientist before nature, see the work of Loren Eiseley.[18] Poetry, as an immediate response to phenomena and the celebration of experience in forms appropriate to what is experienced, is becoming more interesting to both scientist and theologian. The poet (here we use the word broadly) is one who is less interested in the grand scheme and the manipulable object than in responding to what is there: a person, an event, this place. The poet responds before trying to systematize. In fact, the poet's first words are not systemizing at all—though they are ordering—but response. The words are ordered and chastened to express response rather than arrangement, system, or management. The poet relies most often on the synecdochic, allowing the specific thing or experience to become a symbol of a wider or deeper perception. As action springs from worship, what is said by an artist is derived from what is deeply heard. A good example of this enlarged conception of the poetic is the work of Annie Dillard, notably *Pilgrim at Tinker Creek* and *Holy the Firm*.

Our culture may be moving beyond the positivistic reductionism which actually inhibits science, morality, economics, and even politics, moving toward a more poetic sense of the world. The church has a very large stake in this movement, for as Nathan Scott has said, our allies in the preaching of the gospel are not the positivists—those who have it all sewn up—but the open-eyed, awestruck poets.[19]

We would do well as preachers to ask why the popularity of science fiction movies. Can it be because they cater to a thirst for the poetic and are open to worlds undiscovered and to wonder?

Marianne Moore intimates the connection between *what* we experience and *how* we express that experience:

SILENCE

My father used to say
"Superior people never make long visits,"
have to be shown Longfellow's grave
or the glass flowers at Harvard.
Self-reliant like the cat—
that takes its prey to privacy,
the mouse's limp tail hanging like a shoelace from its mouth—
they sometimes enjoy solitude,
and can be robbed of speech
by speech which has delighted them.
The deepest feeling always shows itself in silence;
not in silence, but restraint.
Nor was he insincere in saying, "Make my house your inn."
Inns are not residences.[20]

Can we allow the story of our times to become the context of our preaching . . . intentionally? We have seen that the culture does address itself, and we have suggested that it does so in forms which, although not identical with, are congenial to the judgment and claim of the Word as we understand the Word. And that phenomenon makes it possible for us to declare the grace of the gospel among religious folk, to announce the claims of the Word within the civil and religious establishments, to demonstrate the hope of the gospel to reductionistic pragmatists, and to announce the freedom of Christ among the multitudes for whom "Christian" means conformity and the conventional. Culture, under stress, will here and there open to the gospel, and a culture-bound church will clearly be inadequate for such times. As Hans Küng has put it, we can spend so much of ourselves dusting plastic flowers that we do not have time to cultivate roses!

Let us take one problematic model for appreciating the cultural context in which the gospel is spoken: preaching on the parables of Jesus. Recent scholarship leads us to see that we are closest to the historical Jesus, to his perception of God and the kingdom and to his eschatology, in the parables.[21] But these parables, from their earliest oral transmission and through the process of written redaction, have been modified, moralized, allegorized, and generally softened by their interpreters. Thus stories of Jesus have become admonitions of the ascended Lord, the kingdom has been identified more and more closely with the church, the ways of God have been domesticated, and Jesus' reticence about eschatology has been assimilated to our need to say, "Lo here . . . lo there."

The parables of Jesus emerged from their cultural context, and they reveal a poet's sensitivity. Their power in their original setting was their cultural weight rather than their moral or ecclesial persuasiveness. As Paul Ricoeur says, we will miss the parables altogether if we fail to see that they are frankly profane stories:

> Here resides the initial paradox: on the one hand these stories are—as a critic said—narratives of normalcy; but on the other hand it is the kingdom of God that is said to be like this. . . . It is not the religious man in us, it is not the sacred man in us, but precisely the profane man, the secular man who is summoned.[22]

"It is the secular man who is summoned." In the culture's own terms the parables transcend, address, and challenge the culture. Here is the Stranger who knows how to ask questions. The "picture part" of the parables, as Eta Linnemann calls it, was completely recognizable in Jesus' cultural setting and, on the lips of the parabler, interlocked with popular notions of God, kingdom, morality, and humanity. The more profane, radical, and unassimilable they are, the closer we are to the parables as Jesus spoke them. He challenged the popular culture-religion by knowing it intimately and employing its own images and beliefs.

What happens when we hear the parables today? We may take them as the words of the ascended Lord of the church: we stand up, burn incense, and reverence the priest who reads them with sanctified lips. The Lord of the church, we think, would never have countenanced a double-dealing employee or a boy's leaving his father's farm for fun city. In the first case we rationalize the story to protect Jesus' moral standards, or in the other we focus on the waywardness of the son, moralizing and urging repentance. Either approach may miss the parable's controlling image. We are too religious really to hear the parables, and as preachers we tend too often to use them to reinforce rather than to challenge the culture-religion, for the relativities of our own culture have prevented our truly hearing the parables as they were intended.

For example, the works-righteousness and Protestant ethic which pervade our society, coupled with an ingrained idea of the sacredness of Scripture, will not let us hear very clearly the story of equal pay for unequal work. And we are precisely the people who need to hear it! We meet the parable at the level of economics (as we should, for that is what the story is about)—but then we move quickly (to avoid the offense and any connection between our Lord and economic naiveté) by preaching on the employer's compassion and concern for the unemployed or by stressing the fact that a denarius would in fact sustain a day's living in those times. But we cannot allow Jesus and Holy Scripture to describe God's ways as antithetical to the norms of our culture: "There's no such thing as a free lunch"; "If they want an income, let them work for it!" Could the Lord of the church approve of an employer's arbitrary action? "Never!" we say; we are simply unable to accept the idea, any more than we can hear the story as story, enter into its deep contradiction, and be changed by it. The result is the moralized and allegorized story, flattened out to fit both our social and theological conventions and no longer able to astound or save us.

But just as culture is the place where God is present to us, so Jesus' parables are also "the house of God." Hearing and preaching the parables, therefore, always requires a certain cultural awareness, whichever of two approaches we take. We can on the other hand attempt to recover the cultural environment in which the parables were spoken (and the changing setting which accompanied their redaction). It may be possible to reenter that world by historical imagination and to hear the parable with those who first heard it. A sermon of this kind would provide the congregation with historical and cultural information of the kind which Eta Linnemann provides and then readdress the parable to that situation.

Or alternatively, we may do the necessary historical/critical work and then, moving away from the parable per se, attempt a new parable in terms of our own culture. This is not so much translation as parable evoking parable. Jesus' story actually comes to function, for the preacher and through the preacher for the congregation, to call forth story. Whether one takes this approach or a combination of the two, it is awareness of and openness to culture which allows the parable's picture part, the story, to *interlock* with the "reality part," the story of our times.

Take for example the similitude of the mustard seed (Mark 4:30–32). In the history of its interpretation teachers and preachers have tended to emphasize the meager beginnings of the church, the growth of the Christian mission, the present visible dominions of the church catholic. Because the original context of the parable is lost to us, we cannot be sure what the parabler intended. We are stuck with no more than these words. We can of course learn about the mustard plant, the importance of vegetation and shade in the arid Middle East, and we can keep in mind that this is about Jesus' familiar theme, the kingdom of God. But finally this image of the tiny, potent seed is all we have and, we may add, precisely what we need.

Our cultural predisposition—positivistic, pragmatic, success-oriented—is to reduce the parable to a moralism or a formula: "You can start small and make it big." Or the ecclesiastical context may lead us to institutionalize the parable, to reduce it to a demographic projection: "from twelve to a billion." All of this fits easily into our ways of living. Whose style of life cannot accommodate the idea that "from tiny acorns mighty oaks do grow"? And what is saving in that?

But what if we cannot reduce or assimilate this parable? What if we are caught by the image—the tiny seed lying on the earth—and made to reconsider our lives, even our styles and standards of living? No one can tell us what the parable *means*. As with all the parables, we can only be trapped for meditation and reconsideration, and even repentance, where the story—these very words and images—is given freedom, by the preacher and by the listener who can lean into the language, to save us both through and from the story of our times.

NOTES

1. T. S. Eliot, *The Complete Poems and Plays* (New York: Harcourt, Brace & Co., 1952), p. 103.
2. Cf. Harvey Cox, *The Seduction of the Spirit* (New York: Simon & Schuster, 1971).
3. Dean Hoge, *Division in the Protestant House* (Philadelphia: Westminster Press, 1976).
4. Philip Slater, *The Pursuit of Loneliness: American Culture at the Breaking Point* (Boston: Beacon Press, 1970).
5. Cf. William Butler Yeats, "The Second Coming," in *New Anthology of Modern Poetry,* ed. Selden Rodman (New York: Random House, 1946).
6. John Dominic Crossan, *In Parables* (New York: Harper & Row, Publishers, 1973).
7. Eliot, *The Complete Poems and Plays,* pp. 101-3.
8. David Storey, *The Changing Room* (New York: Avon Books, 1975).
9. Cox, *Seduction of the Spirit.*
10. Robert Penn Warren, *All the King's Men* (New York: Harcourt, Brace & Co., 1947).
11. Cf. Ernest Becker, *The Denial of Death* (New York: Macmillan Publishing Co., The Free Press, 1973).
12. Carmen Bernos DeGastold, *Prayers from the Ark* (New York: Penguin Books, 1976), p. 13.
13. D. L. Coburn, *The Gin Game* (New York: Drama Book Specialists, 1978).
14. Adam Finnerty, *No More Plastic Jesus* (Maryknoll, N.Y.: Orbis Books, 1977), p. 2.
15. Marianne Micks, *The Future Present* (New York: Seabury Press, 1970).
16. Kurt Vonnegut, *Cat's Cradle* (New York: Delacorte Press, 1963), p. 132.
17. Frederick Buechner, "Message in the Stars," in *The Magnificent Defeat* (New York: Seabury Press, 1968), p. 47.
18. Loren Eiseley, *The Immense Journey* (New York: Random House, 1957); idem, *The Firmament of Time* (New York: Atheneum Publishers,

1960); idem, *The Unexpected Universe* (New York: Harcourt, Brace & World, 1969); idem, *The Invisible Pyramid* (New York: Charles Scribner's Sons, 1970).

19. Cf. N. A. Scott, *The Broken Center* (New Haven: Yale University Press, 1966).

20. Marianne Moore, *Poems and Essays: A Marianne Moore Reader* (New York: Viking Press, 1965), p. 22.

21. Cf. Crossan, *In Parables.*

22. Paul Ricoeur, "Listening to the Parables of Jesus," *Criterion,* Spring 1974, pp. 18–22.

4

Focusing
the Listeners' Story

Morris J. Niedenthal

A preacher looks out at the gathered congregation, recognizes many faces, and knows that behind those faces are many diverse stories. A teenage boy whose girl has recently fallen out of love with him sits with head bowed, seemingly unable to look anyone in the face. Three pews behind him is a teenage girl whose sparkling eyes and coy smile tell of her having recently fallen in love. Across the aisle is a physician weary from emergency surgery the night before. At the opposite end of the same pew is a mother with three small children; she is handing them crayons and paper to occupy their attention and keep them still. In the back pew is a man who is convinced that he will never have a job which will enable him to express his real gifts and talents and bring him satisfaction. These are some of the people to whom the sermon must be addressed; the preacher recognizes them all and knows their diverse stories.

Preaching to an assembly of people with different needs and different experiences can be perplexing. For it is clearly impossible to address on Sunday morning any of those five people in a way that deals with the concrete particulars of their several stories. But it has become apparent now that there is a common Story, a shared Story, and that it runs deep in peoples' lives, affecting profoundly the ways in which they feel and think and live.

It isn't enough however for the preacher merely to know in a detached, intellectual way that this Story is a large part of the story of each listener. Rather, each listener must recognize his or her own story in its universal and therefore in its particular dimensions, in what the preacher says. The listener must feel, "Why, that preacher understands what it's like to face what I have to face!" If this recognition is to occur, the preacher must learn how to focus the listener's story so that the listener can recognize it.

We shall consider both some resources and some methods which facilitate this focusing process, and then go on to ask about the identity of the listeners whose story needs to be focused. Note that the technique continues to be largely inductive, moving out from the experiential as the point of contact.

One resource is the simple recognition of the commonality of our human experience—even such experience as evokes emotions which seem very private. Carl Rogers writes, "What is most personal is most general."[1] The same thought can be expressed in different words: "Repeatedly I have found to my astonishment that the feelings which have seemed to be most private, most personal, and therefore the feelings I least expect to be understood by others, when clearly expressed, resonate deeply and consistently with their own experience. This has led me to believe that what I experience in the most unique and personal way, if brought to clear expression, is precisely what others are most deeply experiencing in analogous ways." Who has not had a similar experience—in a group, perhaps, in which someone has finally been able to "get up the nerve to raise that burning question which I thought was troubling only stupid me!"[2]

The biblical traditions are a second resource. These traditions contain stories of God's dealings with his people and their dealings with him. Light shines both ways in the preacher's effort to focus the listeners' story: from the genuinely personal stories we live to the biblical stories, and from the biblical stories to our own stories. Through this process of illumination, preachers focus their listeners' story theologically.

A method or discipline which enables and serves this focusing process is for the preacher to look at the sermon, and to ask who the listeners are and how their story has been focused, according to the content and approach of the sermon. Select four or five people in the congregation whose faces you look into as you preach. Concentrate on them and their lives. Then ask the question, Who am I as the preacher saying these five people are, by virtue of what I say in the sermon? That is a crucial question to answer, and the answer will indicate how I focus my listeners' story and how I address the gospel to them.

Who are these people before me? More specifically, who are the four or five I am concentrating on? People who outwardly are quite confident, competent, comfortable, and contented but who are perhaps inwardly haunted by fear and anxiety? Edmund Steimle asserts, "Scratch the surface of a rich, comfortable, self-righteous pharisee in our churches and you will find an anxious pharisee. Scratch the surface of a narrow, prejudiced deacon or elder and you're likely to find a frightened deacon or elder. Scratch the surface of a rebellious teenager and you'll probably find a scared kid."[3] Which of these—according to the sermon—is that teenager, that elder, that pharisee? And have I dealt with them as they really are?

Fear and anxiety are overpowering dynamics in our modern life. If we believe these dynamics focus our listeners' story, then they will provide the context for our proclamation of that incredibly passionate love which identifies with us even in the extremity of godforsakenness, that love God gives which can overcome and which casts out fear.

Fear, however, dare not be the only focus. Let the suggested discipline move us on to ask again, Who are these people? They are men and women who are subject to the same universal needs that have plagued people for centuries. Regardless of race, age, and civilization, they experience in one form or another strain, struggle, disappointment, the pull of evil, pain, disease, death, and bereavement. These universal human needs, experiences, and emotions have provided the central focus of the church's proclamation over the centuries. The same is true today.

But H. H. Farmer makes a significant observation in this connection.[4] He claims that there are two sets of factors or influences which help to shape the life of every person. One set of factors, as has already been suggested, is that of universal internal needs. But a second set of factors has to do with the external setting of peoples' lives, which includes their social, political, and economic environment. This setting varies; it lacks the permanency and universality that the first set of factors possesses. Farmer concludes that

the situation in relation to the church's message seems to be this. On the one hand, people are today overwhelmingly conscious of the second set of factors [the social, political, and economic arrangements of their life], conscious perhaps as they have never been before. They are still subject to the universal permanent needs of human life, of course, but these largely "come at" them through the social and industrial system of which they are a part, and which, they feel, bitterly aggravates them. . . . This on the one hand.

On the other hand, the church in the past has on the whole concentrated on, specialized in, so to say, the application of its message to the first set of factors—the permanent and universal needs and troubles of individual men and women whatever their situation. . . . The result is that the gospel to multitudes seems, in a way that many would find difficult to put into terms, unreal, remote from the basic and absorbing problems of their life.[5]

(Observe how both sets of factors are treated in the sermon "Two Battles" at the end of this chapter.)

Farmer's conclusion suggests the need to reassess the importance of the universal human needs as the focus of the listeners' story. True, people still experience these needs, but they tend to "come at them through the public setting of their life." Consider again for example the relation between one's own home and family life on the one hand and, on the other, the inevitable statistics on divorce and the newsclips of marches for or against gay rights. To be sure, most preachers do not find it easy to focus on the public setting of human life. Most preachers are probably accustomed to preaching the gospel to the individual person, and the public sector of that person's life becomes the arena for faithful obedience. It comes out like this: "God loves you. Now get out there into the world and show it!" The public sector is not included in the good news. It is the area of obligation, duty, and demand.

Current efforts among biblical scholars and theologians to investigate again the full scope of Jesus' proclamation of the kingdom of God may help us banish from our preaching the dichotomy between the private and the public sectors of life.[6] In particular, the way in which Jesus in his parables deals with human life makes it abundantly clear that for him, human destiny is at stake in ordinary creaturely existence—social, economic, and domestic. That is the matrix of his proclamation of the gracious rule of God, the kingdom of God.

This emphasis, so characteristic of the parables, leads to another assessment of the people before the preacher and to another way of focusing the listeners' story. The hearers are people who are engaged in an almost endless number of ordinary creaturely operations and transactions. They think, design, sell, assemble, transport, fabricate, refine. They dig and extract. They plow, plant, cultivate, harvest. They shop, buy, cook, clean, entertain. They argue, defend, bargain, invest, relax. They operate. And these very operations are constitutive of peoples' self-understanding. Ask a salesman who he is, and he will probably answer by telling you what he sells. Moreover, many people exhibit a confidence in their competency to negotiate and master their operations. Many of them can really do pretty much what they choose to do.

How can these people, with these stories, hear the gospel of the grace of God? Joseph Sittler responded to this question: "It has recently been remarked that whereas we have a gospel for the alienated, the hurt, the depressed, the defeated, we have not a gospel for the well, the effective, the joyous, busy, engaged people of this world. And while, to be sure, a gospel that has no word to desolation is no gospel at all, it is more and more widely true that a gospel whose scope does not address people in their joyous, creative, constructive, and effectual operations is unchallenging because uninteresting."[7]

To focus on operationally competent people and to broaden the scope of the gospel, as Sittler suggests, will involve some fundamental changes in the mind-set of many preachers. This change will be featured in the liberation of preachers from the notion that in order to speak or hear the gospel one must first experience frustration, collapse, defeat, and failure. We preachers seem sometimes to be constitutionally programmed to snoop around in people's lives until we can spot their weakness, their sin, their ambiguity of motive and their hypocrisy, as though we could not otherwise speak the gospel to them. It may well be, of course, that the fabric of our culture and of the assumptions that undergird it can be seen to be coming open at the seams here and there and that these openings are openings for the Word. But that does not necessarily mean that the life of an individual can be addressed by the Word only in his or her Achilles' heel. Yet somehow we preachers, on occasion at least, seem more at home with failure than success, sorrow than joy, frustration than achievement. We can become overzealous in reminding people not to think more highly of themselves than they ought, not realizing that St. Paul probably would willingly have added, nor more lowly of themselves than they ought. Some people get the impression that preachers are telling them, "You are really nobodies before God, worthless sinners. Now get out there and be somebodies—for God and his Christ!" You cannot fairly take that impression from the sermon at the end of this chapter, in which the preacher gives his hearers full credit for their competence and their promise.

Suppose for example that one of the women in your congregation is a competent and compassionate physician. Suppose that she also has some strange and prejudiced attitudes toward certain minority groups. Must you first expose her prejudice and sin before you can find a focus for the gospel? Does the gospel have nothing to say about her competency and compassion? Would not the gospel in its fullness actually address the whole person, that is, both her competency and her sin? If what she hears does not address both, can it be the gospel of Jesus Christ?

Preachers need to be liberated from their singular preoccupation with limits, failures, and sins. They can for example entertain and feature God's appreciation, his nod of approval, for that is part of the gospel too. It is expressed for example in the parable of the talents. The spotlight focuses on the one-talent man who has buried his talent and stands trembling before his master. Jesus speaks harsh words to this bloke who made a hobby of his insignificance. But there are other characters in the parable who risk and invest, who become competent and skilled investors, and Jesus speaks to them also. To them he says, "Well done, thou good and faithful servant!"

Recall again now those four or five people you are concentrating on. Who are they in relation to your preaching? How do you focus their story? Are they people who are anxious and fearful? Are they people who are struggling with the universal needs and problems of all human beings regardless of time or place? Or are they people who are deeply involved in the public affairs of their life, engaged in a number of operations, and really quite competent? Who are they?

Before answering prematurely, we need to ask from another angle. We need now to ask whether the biblical stories tell us anything about who they are. Most of the listeners in a congregation have heard some of those stories and have even heard them interpreted by preachers. They probably already know that Jesus died for their sins and the sins of humankind. They probably know they ought to be "more committed to Christ," whatever that means. They probably know that they ought to respond more lovingly and responsibly to their neighbors in need. None of these preachments will probably be earthshaking news to the listener.

The crucial issue, however, is not so much what the listener knows but what the listener believes. And for purposes of nurturing faith, it is important for the preacher to recognize that the biblical stories are told to the people of God. These people are not always a faithful and obedient people, to be sure, but they are nevertheless the people of God. And the biblical stories were told to them only as such. This fact poses a decisive question for preachers in their attempt to focus the listeners' story: are they already sons and daughters of God through Jesus Christ? Or must they be converted, made to be Christians, through the preaching of the gospel?

This question gets to the heart of Christian identity. In what does that identity consist? In a person's works, in a decision for Christ, or in Christlike behavior? Or does it consist in the grace of God in Christ Jesus, which a person acknowledges and receives in faith? Unfortunately, the issue of Christian identity is clouded with confusion. Ask people in our congregations what the word *Christian* means to them. More often than not one is likely to hear, "Christian is what I ought to be, what I try to be," and therefore by implication, "what I am not." This response reflects an understanding of Christian faith not as bestowing an identity but as demanding one. It consists in obeying the law, in doing the "oughts," as though one really were justified by works. (St. Paul must be squirming in his grave!) Small wonder therefore that many people look upon the Christian life as demanding, burdensome, and exhausting—with little joy and gladness. After all, it demands an identity but does not offer one.

The biblical stories present a radically different viewpoint. Identity for the people of God consists in God's action, his calling, and his faithfulness even unto death. The identity of Israel owes nothing to Israel's behavior or performance; Israel is given its identity by God. The Christian communities likewise are given an identity by God through Jesus Christ. Why is it that our Jewish sisters and brothers appear more ready to say, "I am a Jew," than we are to say, "I am a Christian." Perhaps we need to listen more closely to them; perhaps we can learn from them that our identity consists in God's action, not our own. (On the technical implications of this discussion for hermeneutics, see chapter 8 below.)

That explains why the biblical stories are told to, and about, the people of God even when they are wayward and disobedient. Moreover, it explains why the mood and plot of many of the stories can be described as a lover's quarrel. Robert Frost wrote, "I had a lover's quarrel with the world."⁸ That image of a lover's quarrel aids us in following the movement and inner dynamic of the biblical stories. "Lover" implies a yearning and longing for the beloved, a commitment and bond between them, an emptiness and incompleteness without the other, a deep and abiding affirmation of the other. "Quarrel," on the other hand, signifies controversy, contention, dispute, a break in friendly relations often caused by love spurned or perverted, and the subsequent need for confrontation. Affirmation and confrontation—these are the two aspects of a lover's quarrel.

The biblical stories repeatedly tell of God's having a lover's quarrel with his people. Hosea describes the agony Yahweh feels because of his disappointed love:

> When Israel was a child, I loved him,
>   and out of Egypt I called my son.
> The more I called them,
>   the more they went from me.
> they kept sacrificing to the Baals,
>   and burning incense to idols.
>
> Yet it was I who taught Ephraim to walk,
>   I took them up in my arms;
>   but they did not know that I healed them.
> I led them with cords of compassion,
>   with the bands of love,
> and I became to them as one
>   who eases the yoke on their jaws,
>   and I bent down to them and fed them.
>
> How can I give you up, O Ephraim!
>   How can I hand you over, O Israel!
> How can I make you like Admah!
>   How can I treat you like Zeboiim!
> My heart recoils within me,
>   my compassion grows warm and tender.
> I will not execute my fierce anger,
>   I will not again destroy Ephraim;
> for I am God and not man,
>   the holy One in your midst,
>   and I will not come to destroy.
>   (Hos. 11:1-4, 8-9)

But the stories also tell of the lover's quarrel the people had with Yahweh. Abraham had his quarrel with God, as did Jacob and Job,

Elijah and Jeremiah. Add New Testament figures too: A Syrophoenician woman, Jesus, and Paul. Consider for example the quarrel which Abraham, our father in the faith, waged with the Lord. Sensing the injustice that would be perpetrated if the Lord destroyed Sodom and Gomorrah, killing both righteous and unrighteous people, Abraham asked, " 'Shall not the Judge of all the earth do right?' And the Lord said, 'If I find at Sodom fifty righteous in the city, I will spare the whole place for their sake.' " Abraham keeps pressing his case before the Lord, moving from forty-five to thirty to twenty. Then he says, " 'Oh let not the Lord be angry, and I will speak again but this once. Suppose ten are found.' He answered, 'For the sake of ten I will not destroy it.' And the Lord went his way, when he had finished speaking to Abraham; and Abraham returned to his place" (Gen. 18:22–33).

The relationship between God and his people, as exemplified by the story of Abraham's haggling, is intensely interpersonal and dynamic. That helps explain why it is described through stories—stories whose motivating energy is a lover's quarrel. Moreover, this deeply interpersonal relationship between God and his people guides us in understanding more comprehensively God's will for his people, and his claim on them. "What is the chief end of man?" The *Westminster Catechism* answers its own first question: "To glorify God and to enjoy him forever." To "enjoy" God suggests an affectional, a lover's relationship. Contrast that relationship with the one posited in a military analogy, in which the catechetical response would read, "To glorify God and to obey him forever."

Understanding of the will of God can surely be expressed more appropriately in terms of the lover courting and wooing the beloved than in terms of the commander rapping out orders. Robert Capon presses the analogy further:

> The will of God now becomes . . . the longing of a lover for what the beloved is. It is a desire, not for a performance, but for a person; a wish, not that the beloved will be obedient, but that she will be herself—the self that is already loved to distraction. The will of God, seen this way, is not *in order to* something, but *because* of someone. . . . Let us make ourselves a promise to talk for a while about the will of God as attractive rather than coercive, as a delighting more than a deciding.[9]

The images of a lover and his beloved and of the lover's quarrel aid us not only in following the biblical stories but also in focusing the listeners' story. God's lover's quarrel with his people continues. He continues to affirm and confront his people in order to create them anew into what they were intended to be. Both God's affirmation and his confrontation are rooted in his passionate love. He accepts people as they are but he will never leave them as they are just because he loves them. An analogy might clarify the point. It would obviously be a failure of love to insist that an alcoholic amend his ways and stop drinking before a person would accept him and relate to him genuinely. Love accepts a person as he or she is. But it would equally be a failure of love to accept an alcoholic as he is and be unconcerned about his changing his life-style. Love does not leave a person on a path of self-destruction. So with God and his relationship with his people. He accepts them as they are but will not leave them as they are—just because he loves them and has in mind for them nothing less than a new creation.

How, one might ask, does the lover's quarrel continue today among the listeners to preaching? What in their stories might express this relationship with God? Attend to the frustration people experience when they encounter limits to their own self-willing determination. Teachers sometimes feel frustrated when they can no longer impose their wills and desires on a class of students. The class constitutes a limit to a teacher's will to have his or her own way. Parents have similar experiences with their children. They feel frustrated and sometimes helpless when their children will no longer do what they want them to do. They have encountered a limit to their own wills. Americans were frustrated when the United States could not impose its will on Vietnam. The Vietnamese people were a limit to the self-willing determination of the American nation. Experiences of limits usually cause frustration. But they are one of God's strategies in his lover's quarrel with us to keep us human.

Attend to the claims for justice which are laid on people by others and which sometimes create fear. A husband crawls out of bed at seven A.M., feels like jumping back into bed, but instead shaves, dresses, and heads off to work—not necessarily because he wants to but because he has some elementary sense of justice. His wife and kids have a right to expect justice from him as head of the household. Oppressed people in our own country and around the world are clamoring for justice, for human rights. And in some neighborhoods these shouts for justice provoke fear, especially among the people who already enjoy justice. These claims for justice, and even these fears, are dynamics in God's lover's quarrel with us to make life humane for all people.

Attend to the gladness of heart which comes through acceptance and affirmation. A son runs toward his father, leaps into the father's outstretched arms and squeezes his own tiny arms around his father's chest. The father feels glad and proud. Think of the affirmation that comes from work well done, works of hand and voice and mind. A meal well prepared and graciously served. An old house tastefully refurbished and refurnished. A legal case well argued and well defended. A musical composition carefully interpreted and gracefully played. Gladness of heart that comes from work well done. There is also that acceptance which is totally undeserved. An undeserved word of forgiveness is spoken and it opens a new relationship and a new possibility for life together. Those stirrings of a glad heart are godly signs that in his lover's quarrel with us God still regards us as being worthwhile, his beloved children.

Attend to the energies of hope which enable people to pick up their lives and start living and loving again. A woman suffering from a lingering illness knows her future life will consist of diminished activity. Yet she now has time to do things she had always wanted to do and never had time to do before. "Life is good," she says. A man is suddenly released from his job and, being unable to secure a similar job in another company, begins to prepare for a career he had never dreamed of. Another man, knowing all too well, through his wife's death, the pain of loving, nevertheless begins to love another woman. God kindles the flames of hope in his lover's quarrel with us to keep us from resigning ourselves to present circumstances and to despair.

But attend also to the lover's quarrel people today still have with God. Some will be expressed orally; others will be carried in the secret of one's own heart. A mother cries, "Where were you, Lord, when my only son was run over by an automobile and killed?" A teenager is confused: if she stands up for what she thinks is right and decent, she will probably be ostracized from the group she associates with. A manager loses a promotion for speaking out against an unfair company policy. "What is going on, Lord?" "Where are you, Lord?" "What are you doing, Lord?" "For God's sake, answer!"—so the people question and cry in their lover's quarrel with God in an effort to hold him accountable.

One last time we ask, Who are these people before the preacher?

Ultimately, they are brothers and sisters of Jesus, God's children, who are caught up in their lover's quarrel with God and his lover's quarrel with them. Some preachers may disagree with this definition. After all, they say, many of my listeners do not respond and act like brothers and sisters of Jesus. But "remember Max Beerbohm's Happy Hypocrite, the wicked man who wore the mask of a saint to woo and win the saintly girl he loved. Years later when a castoff girl friend discovered the ruse, she challenged him to take off the mask in front of his beloved and show his face for the sorry thing it was. He did what he was told only to discover that underneath the saint's mask, his face had become the face of a saint."[10]

Relate to the listeners as saints, and maybe—just maybe—they will become saintly!

NOTES

1. Carl Rogers, *On Becoming a Person* (New York: Houghton Mifflin Co., 1961), p. 26.

2. Thomas Oden, *The Structure of Awareness* (Nashville: Abingdon Press, 1969), pp. 23-24.

3. Edmund Steimle, "Preaching out of Season," Thesis Theological Cassettes, vol. 2, no. 1 (Pittsburgh: 1972).

4. H. H. Farmer, *The Servant of the Word* (Philadelphia: Fortress Press, 1964).

5. Ibid., pp. 85-86.

6. Cf. Norman Perrin, *Jesus and the Language of the Kingdom* (Philadelphia: Fortress Press, 1976).

7. Joseph Sittler, *The Anguish of Preaching* (Philadelphia: Fortress Press, 1966), p. 38.

8. Robert Frost, *The Poetry of Robert Frost* (New York: Holt, Rinehart & Winston, 1967), p. 355.

9. Robert Farrar Capon, *Hunting the Divine Fox* (New York: Seabury Press, 1974), p. 38.

10. Frederick Buechner, *Wishful Thinking* (New York: Harper & Row, Publishers, 1973), p. 52.

The Two Battles

Frederick Buechner

Finally, be strong in the Lord and in the strength of his might. Put on the whole armor of God, that you may be able to stand against the wiles of the devil. For we are not contending against flesh and blood, but against the principalities, against the powers, against the world rulers of this present darkness, against the spiritual hosts of wickedness in the heavenly places. Therefore take the whole armor of God, that you may be able to withstand in the evil day, and having done all, to stand. Stand therefore, having girded your loins with truth, and having put on the breastplate of righteousness, and having shod your feet with the equipment of the gospel of peace; above all taking the shield of faith, with which you can quench all the flaming darts of the evil one. And take the helmet of salvation, and the sword of the Spirit, which is the word of God. Pray at all times in the Spirit, with all prayer and supplication.

Ephesians 6:10–18

St. Paul, or whoever it was who wrote this letter, was not the first to speak of life as a battle, nor was he the last; but familiar and hackneyed as the metaphor has become, it is also true. To grow, to move, to become, is to wage war against many adversaries. Most of

[Frederick Buechner, *The Magnificent Defeat* (New York: Seabury Press, 1966).]

the time it is an undeclared war. We do not announce publicly what we are fighting for or what we are fighting against or why we think that it is worth the fight, and very often we do not know the answer to these questions ourselves; but a kind of war is nonetheless what we are all engaged in, and the history of each individual no less than the history of nations rings loud with the tumult of it—advances and retreats, truces and delaying actions, here a victory, there a defeat, all of it. Even in the silence of a church, for instance: the preacher advances, his tattered banners flying—maybe even God advances—and what do we do? Surrender? Retreat behind our shields? Launch some kind of counterattack of the heart, the mind? Who knows. But whatever we do, to live is to do battle under many different flags, and of all our battles, there are two, I believe, that are major ones.

The first is a war of conquest, which is a war to heat the blood of even the most timorous, because one way or another we all fight to conquer, and what we fight to conquer is the world. Not literally the world, perhaps, although like Walter Mitty we may dream a little in that direction sometimes; but for the most part our goal is a more realistic one: just a place in the world, a place in the sun, our place. And that takes fighting too, of course. All our lives we fight for a place in the sun—not a place in the shadows where we fear getting lost in the shadows and becoming a kind of shadow ourselves, obscure and unregarded. There are so many lives like that. We walk down the streets of a city—not just the poorer streets either—and the faces come at us like dead leaves in the wind, one face so much like another in its emptiness and defeat that it takes the most concentrated effort to see it as a human face at all, unique, individual, like the face of no other human being who has ever lived or will live. These are the invisible men of our world; we look at them without really seeing them. We fight to be *visible,* to move into a place in the sun, a place in the family, the community, in whatever profession we choose, a place where we can belong, where there is light enough to be recognized as a person and to keep the shadows at bay. The Germans use the word *lebensraum,* room to live in. We feel that we must conquer a territory in time and space that will be ours. And that is true. We must.

If that is the goal of this war of conquest that we all must wage, there are also the adversaries with whom we have to wage it; and they are adversaries of flesh and blood. They are human beings like ourselves, each of whom is fighting the same war toward the same end and under a banner emblazoned with the same word that our banners bear, and that word is of course Myself, or Myself and my Family, or Myself and my Country, Myself and my Race, which are all really MYSELF writ large. It can be the most ruthless of all wars, but on the other hand it need not be. Saints and sinners fight it both. Genghis Khan fought such a war under such a banner, but so does Martin Luther King. It can be the naked war of the jungle, my ambition against your ambition, my will against your will, or it can be war more in the sense of the knight at arms who abides by the rules of chivalry. If often it is the war of the unjust against the just, it can also be a war of the just against the unjust. But whichever it is, it is the war of flesh against flesh: to get ahead, to win, to gain or regain power, to survive in a world where not even survival is had without struggle.

To use the metaphor of Ephesians, what is the armor to wear in such a war? Not, certainly, the whole armor of God here but, rather, the whole armor of man, because this is a man's war against other men. In such a war, perhaps, you wear something like this. Gird your loins with wisdom, the sad wisdom of the world which knows that dog eats dog, that the gods help those who help themselves and charity begins at home. Put on the breastplate of self-confidence because if you have no faith in yourself, if you cannot trust to your own wits, then you will never get anywhere. Let your feet be shod with the gospel of success—the good news that you can get just about anything in this world if you want it badly enough and are willing to fight for it. Above all, take the shield of security, because in a perilous world where anything can happen, security is perhaps what you need more than anything else—the security of money in the bank, or a college degree, or some basic skill that you can always fall back on. And take the helmet of attractiveness or personality and the sword of wit. People are always criticizing the advertising business for its implied promise that the one who gets the best job or the prettiest girl is the one who wears the right clothes or uses the right toothpaste or drinks the right brand of vodka. But the fact of the matter is that although this is by no means a happy truth about our society, it is nonetheless very often not far from being true. In a world where the competition is fierce, to dress well, to be able to speak well on your feet, to be good at games, may actually make the difference between winning and losing. In the war of conquest, that is to say, in the war that we all wage for a place in the sun, it is the armor of man rather than the armor of God that will serve you best; and although I cannot value that armor as highly as some would value it, I also cannot mock it, because the armor of man serves its purpose all too well, and because I wear some of it myself, and so do you.

But there is another war that we fight, of course, all of us, and this one is not a war against flesh and blood. "For we are not contending against flesh and blood," the letter reads. Then against what? What worse is there to contend against in this world than other men? "The principalities . . . the powers . . . the world rulers of this present darkness . . . the spiritual hosts of wickedness in the heavenly places," Paul writes. "The wiles of the devil." This language is so foreign to modern thinking and so offensive to modern ears that when this famous passage is read at commencements and baccalaureates every year, I suspect that most people tend not really to hear it. They listen to the magnificent description of the whole armor of God that I have parodied and wrenched out of shape, and to the degree that they think about it at all, my guess is that they marvel at what stirring and beautiful words these are to address to the young as they prepare to step forth into the battle of life, and let it go at that.

But unless I am mistaken, the battle of life that they have in mind, and certainly the battle of life that most of the young have in mind, is the battle that I have tried to describe, the battle to get ahead. But in that battle, surely, the armor of God, which the letter catalogs, is not only of precious little use but will almost certainly prove an encumbrance. If any of us are battering our heads against the opposition of men, it is not the helmet of salvation that we need. If it is a higher place in the pecking order that we want, we can dispense with the sword of the Spirit. But what then is this other great war in which the armor of God, and only the armor of God, can see us through? What is this other great war that all of us wage in which it is the armor of man that becomes useless and sometimes worse than useless? There is no man, I believe, who does not know the answer.

This other war is the war not to conquer but the war to become whole and at peace inside our skins. It is a war not of conquest now but of liberation, because the object of this other war is to liberate that dimension of selfhood which has somehow become lost, that dimension of selfhood that involves the capacity to forgive and to will the good not only of the self but of all other selves. This other war is the war to become a human being. This is the goal that we are really after and that God is really after. This is the goal that power, success, and security are only forlorn substitutes for. This is the victory that not all our human armory of self-confidence and wisdom and personality can win for us—not simply to be treated as human but to become at last truly human.

To describe our enemy in this war, the one that we must fight to liberate ourselves from, Paul writes of the devil—"the wiles of the devil"—and our age cringes at the word. But perhaps his word "darkness" will do. That is what we have to be set free from—the darkness in ourselves that we never fully see or fully understand or feel fully responsible for, although heaven knows we are more than a little responsible. The science of psychology has its own vocabulary of darkness—trauma, psychosis, death-wish—but Paul says it so that a child could understand: "I do not do the good I want, but the evil I do not want is what I do." And it is also the evil in the world that the world does not want. No one but a madman, for instance, wants to blow up the world, but we live at a time when some of the sanest and wisest men on both sides of the iron curtain may decide to do just that. No one but a madman would will the mountains of the dead on the beaches of Normandy, at Auschwitz, Hiroshima, Vietnam, but there they lie. Call it what you will, the evil in this world is greater than the sum of all human evil, which is great enough, just as the evil in ourselves as individuals is greater than the evil that we choose, and that is great enough too. This is the darkness that we need to be liberated from in order to become human. This is what the great war of liberation is all about. "Wretched man that I am! Who will deliver me from this body of death?" This is the cry at the heart of every man and at the heart of the world.

It is for this war, not the other one, that we need the whole armor of God. We must gird our loins with truth, and for us, in the end, there is only truth, and it is the Christ. He is the truth about who man really is, about what it means to be really human, and about who God really is. And his cross is the truth about what the darkness is, in us and in our world; and his cross is the truth about what the love of God is, in us and in our world. We must put on the breastplate of righteousness, and righteousness in the last analysis is love—not love as an emotion necessarily but love as an act of the will: love as the act of willing another's good even though we may despise the darkness in him just as we will our own good even though we despise the darkness in ourselves. It is not until we love a person in all his ugliness that we can make him beautiful, or ourselves either. Above all, we must take the shield of faith, and faith here is not so much believing this thing or that thing about God as it is hearing a voice that says, "Come unto me." We hear the voice, and then we start to go without really knowing what to believe either about the voice or about ourselves; and yet we go. Faith is standing in the darkness, and a hand is there, and we take it.

And finally, of course, we must "pray at all times in the Spirit . . . making supplication for all the saints and also for me." In the great war of liberation, it is imperative to keep in touch always with the only one who can liberate. We must speak to him however hard it may be in the thick of the fight, however irrelevant it may sometimes seem, however dried up and without faith we may feel. And we must not worry too much about the other war, the war of conquest. Of course to some extent we must worry about it, and it is necessary and right that we should. But in the war for a place in the sun, we must never mistake conquest for final victory, and above all, we must never mistake failure for final defeat. Because even if we do not find our place in the sun, or not quite the place we want, or a place where the sun is not as bright as we always dreamed that it would be, this is not the end because this is not really the decisive war, even though we spend so much of our lives assuming that it is. The decisive war is the other one—to become fully human, which means to become compassionate, honest, brave. And this is a war against the darkness which no man fights alone. It is the war which every man can win who wills to win because it is the war which God also wills us to win and will arm us to win if only we will accept his armor.

PART THREE

THE CHURCHLY CONTEXT

5

Preaching from a Liturgical Perspective

Gilbert E. Doan, Jr.

It is a rare treatise on preaching today which does not insist, early, late, and properly, that the sermon take account of "where the people are." But how often does a treatise on preaching take very seriously where the people quite literally are at the moment the sermon is preached? Or what they have come there to do? Or what they are as a matter of fact actually doing at the moment—namely, praising God?[1] Preaching must be related to that too.

What is this thing which the people are doing—this rite, these ceremonies, this "cult," this phenomenon called worship or liturgy? It is a measure of the intellectualism and rationalism to which the church has been reduced that we are so rarely able to see worship as anything more than "the preliminaries."[2] Yet this sometimes inscrutable and often indigestible interplay of human words and human movements has been in progress since the dawn of human consciousness and will continue, for that matter, in church and out, in the market and on the field, in the hall and at the table, as well as in the sanctuary. It will continue moreover with a high degree of independence, indeed, of insouciance with respect to what is said about it—even by its own cult figures and even in the context of its own ceremonies. Women and men, because they are human beings, *will enact* corporately and in regular ways their responses to those things, persons, or values which they perceive to be ultimate. It is part and parcel of the style of our creation that we respond in rite and ceremony to what we perceive to be ultimate. And that preacher who ignores the ritual and ceremonial matrix in which the sermon is set and that sermon which is perceived to be in basic conflict with the cult are at best no better advised than King Canute's attempt to hold back the waves and tides of the sea.

Does this conception of worship appear to demean Christian liturgy? Does it seem to reduce worship to the level of anthropological crudities of the sort for which children used to pillage the *National Geographic*? By no means! It is a matter of no small consequence theologically that the cult is redeemed by the work of the Spirit of God, and homiletically and liturgically that the motifs of the cult of the redeemed are those of penitence, gratitude, celebration, and ethical consecration rather than those of terror and magic, propitiation and clout. The cult, like the believer, is (and is being) redeemed body and soul by the death and resurrection of Jesus Christ and by the Spirit. But it is nonetheless a profoundly and fundamentally human phenomenon, and one whose human dimensions the preacher ignores only at peril. To put a more constructive face on it, the cultic matrix is one more context to which the preacher must pay disciplined and sensitive attention from the very earliest stages of the hermeneutical task.

What, then, are some characteristics of the Christian cult? Are there characteristics which hold special meaning for those preachers who are able to understand their task in terms of story and the sharing of stories?

There are indeed. First of all, worship in the church of Christ is specifically oriented and specifically addressed. It does not celebrate life, or religious insight, or kindness, or secularity, or community, or authenticity, or any other abstraction, no matter how fashionable. Or even story. It is shaped rather by the surd data of the gospel, which *are* narrative, and is addressed to the creating, redeeming, and sanctifying God who was made flesh in Jesus, who was executed, who was raised from the dead, and who by the power of the Spirit is present in worship. It is a matter of no small consequence that the order of worship conforms basically to that Story—perhaps more clearly in the so-called liturgical churches, but also in the sacramental services of those churches called "free": whether by tradition, instinct, or careful pastoral analysis, there is provided for the worshipers first a period or module of information, instruction, and edification by Scripture and sermon (which corresponds to the earthly ministry of Jesus), and then second the Lord's Supper (which remembers, rehearses, and recapitulates the night in which he was betrayed and carries the paschal mystery through its consummation to the ascension and the promise of his coming again). Thus it is that quite apart from the content of particular component texts and ceremonial acts, the basic spine and form of the Christian service of worship are given in and by the Story of Jesus Christ.

Not only does the order of service regularly recapitulate in this way the Story of Jesus; it also regularly forms that story in the worshiper and the congregation, conforming their common story and their several stories to his. A "repetitive" order of worship, predictable a week or a year in advance, may seem tedious. That is a great pity and a clear indication that the rite is being mishandled. The point of the matter is that properly handled, a repetitive pattern has an enormous if sometimes subliminal power of formation. The Madison Avenue analogue is called "redundancy." By whatever name, it affects behavior and, used on the airwaves, it sells. If it did not it would surely be abandoned.

There are analogues other than the commercial. One of them deserves special attention not only because it is more compatible with the values of the church but also because it centers on repeated physical movement rather than on the reiteration of a slogan. It is a therapeutic procedure, developed within the past few decades, to which the name of *patterning* has been given—and the name is suggestive also of what should happen in weekly worship. The story of therapeutic patterning is briefly as follows: Some infants are born with a certain kind of brain damage. It becomes evident after a certain time that such a child will not make normal behavioral progress—may never even learn to crawl. Drugs and other therapies have been tried in the past but to no avail, and there had long been a disappointed consensus in hopelessness. Then, under the impulse of whatever fury of anger or tenderness of love or instinct of therapeutic imagination, the notion of patterning was conceived and applied. Nurses, therapists, family, and friends took turns endlessly moving the infant's arms and legs in the pattern of the crawl—until after days, weeks, months, the child finally "learned" to crawl on its own.

Now however clinically imprecise the description may be, the basic therapeutic style can only suggest the enormous formational power of a rite whose pattern is both clear and persistently employed. Well handled, the patterning process forms the patterned story into the stories of those who are being (liturgically) patterned. His Story becomes more and more their stories—and story—as theirs becomes, and become, more fully his. It will be well for the preacher in design and delivery to work with this dynamic pattern rather than against it.[3]

Let us turn now to a consideration of the sacraments of the church, which are among the major features of liturgical patterning. Although the sacraments constitute quite properly the explicit focus of some of the work of preaching, it is not intended that much attention be given here to how to preach on, or "preaching values" in, Holy Baptism or Holy Communion. The point here is rather to mark the thoroughly sacramental character of all Christian worship and to derive from that observation some notes for the preaching task. By *sacramental* in this context is meant that worship employs body as well as mind, things as well as ideas, movement and physical property—light, space, color— as well as abstraction and logic, as vehicles both of the Word and of the worship of God. And the implications are manifold and enormous. Only a few can be considered here.[4]

Consider first the words employed by the preacher. Consider them however not as the mere bearers of cognitive freight or instruments of an art form but as the sacramental *materia*. It is ironic indeed that in these very days of heightened public sensitivity, in church and out, to the respectful and faithful handling of light, color, texture, taste, and movement—and in church, to everything from liturgical architecture and dance to the making of banners and the baking of an ecclesiastically proper loaf—the art and craft of words has largely been neglected. This is unfortunate, for

> in preaching, then, we are offering a sacrament. The preacher has not the same preparation to make as the priest. But it is not a less serious task to handle words in the name of God than to offer to men [and to women] the Bread and Wine. . . . There is no sufficient plea to be offered by the man who uses words in a coarse and slipshod way. He is like a graceless priest who treats with flippancy the elements which are holy to him. Something might come on the wings of words, and it does not come because he has been false to his calling. Something incommunicable might be carried in this way; things audible might become signs of things which ear has not heard, but the priest of this sacrament has been false to his trust.[5]

So much, then, for a new respect for words as the elements of a truly sacramental action. Let us turn to another major implication of the sacramental character of worship. If preaching is to be an integral part of such worship, the preachers are obliged thereby to regard as a matter of ultimate spiritual consequence—rather than as an incidental, a matter of mere human limitation or a regrettable complication—the handling and use of their own bodies in the act of preaching. Failure to do so can be catastrophic. It was once this writer's privilege to participate in a team-taught course in homiletics. The assignment given to one of the members of the team was to analyze the mechanics of delivery: posture, gesture, carriage, pause and timing, facial expression, and breath control. This exegete, though his assignment seemed limited, could demonstrate conclusively, by judicious postmortem caricature, whether the preacher for the day had done the work he felt obliged to do, believed what he preached, felt it worth saying, and trusted or respected the listeners. It was uncanny—yet, when demonstrated to an otherwise fairly cerebral class, so obvious! And so important![6]

The preacher's physical behavior has further consequences, which cannot here be considered at length. Let it suffice to note briefly two additional examples. First, it is easy for a worshiper to determine, from the preacher's own attentiveness or intensity or animation or tone of voice or "bending," where the preacher thinks "the action is" liturgically and whether the psalms or the prayers or the distribution (or the anthem, for that matter) are there merely to be got through. Second, if the preacher decides to use the pulpit when the sermon is derived from a passage in which the Lord "has a controversy with his people" but chooses to perambulate the center aisle for a sermon on the text "a rest remaineth," the dissonance implicit in such choices will not be lost on the hearers, whether or not they recognize the dissonance or can put words to it.[7]

As could be inferred from the foregoing, a liturgical text or ceremonial act can be taken in itself as the explicit focus of the sermon. In the course of a year's preaching, the preacher will choose appropriate occasions to illuminate the liturgy by the exposition of the text, or to use a rite of the church to illustrate or illuminate the text. The sensitive preacher will be able to weave into the sermon, almost in throwaway fashion, the images, phrases, words, and figures of the liturgy in order to strengthen the connections between the two. By the same token the preacher will avoid conflicts in imagery—choosing for example some Sunday other than Pentecost to describe hell in terms of fire. Look at the sermon below entitled "The Eye of the Storm." Can you imagine participating in the service at which that sermon was preached? Would "All is calm, all is bright" ever be the same again?

The liturgical preacher will find occasion to illuminate ceremonial acts as well as texts. The sermon may not be *about* the "journey to the center of the earth," or even employ the phrase, but a sensitive exegete of ceremony will realize that whether a trip to the chancel be to present the offering, to receive the bread and wine, or to answer an altar call, that "journey" is far older than the Christian community and is heavy with destiny and mystery for those who take it. And if a candidate is to be baptized, or a class confirmed, the opportunity is there for the preacher to begin each sentence of one paragraph with "As you make your way to the altar . . ." and thus, by attention to ceremony, interpret and empower the whole event.

Consider a Christmas Eve sermon, similar to "The Eye of the Storm"—in which the text is not "All is calm" but the act of lighting the candles. What new fire might an adult believer receive—or strike—or see—on Christmas Eve?

And surely in relation to the central realities of passion and resurrection, as they are exposed and enacted in baptism and the Eucharist, the ritual and ceremonial loose ends must be forever and repeatedly caught up in the preaching—not all at once but over the years, with the relentlessness that comes of a determination to put first things first, of an appreciation for the uses of redundancy and patterning, and of the desire to mine for their riches for faith rather than to ignore or minimize the structures and dynamics of these rites.

The question has already been raised several times, Who is speaking in the sermon, the preacher, the congregation, or the Lord? The question is not answered simply. As has been implied in the foregoing chapters, and as chapter 10 will disclose further, the preaching of the Word in the congregation is a profoundly dialogical matter. This matter cannot here be explored at length, but it must be recognized that the dialogical character of the sermon has liturgical ramifications which deserve brief consideration. To several of these we now turn.

If one part of a true dialogue or conversation, for example, is listening, another attending, another considering, another relishing, another understanding, and another "applying," then the use of silence, especially after the lessons and immediately before the sermon (which is clearly the way in which they should be placed in relation to each other), is highly appropriate. It is useful as well following the sermon. True liturgical silence does not come easily to American congregations. It must be researched and explained, introduced, and patiently practiced and learned. But once learned, the silence before the Word tends to show up our accustomed lack of silence as sheer disrespect. A respectful and appropriate silence is an important component of an offering of worship. And perhaps as a test of the dialogical character of the sermon, the minister should ask before preaching, Is this a sermon which it will be appropriate to surround with the silence of the believer before the Word?

Although the sermon may well be of a kind which it is appropriate to frame within such silence, and although it may, by the power of the Spirit, be the Word of God to a hearer, it is nonetheless an artifact of the preacher's creation. It will be well, therefore, for the preacher to regard the sermon itself as a part of the response of faith rather than as the address from on high, in the divine-human dialogue—as an offering, that is, tendered with the preacher's own hand, but nonetheless in solidarity with the whole community of believers.

On the other hand, however, in fashioning and preparing the sermon for its offering, the preacher must remember that Almighty God does speak to men and women through sermons, too! And that is a divine-human dialogue. Hence the conundrum! You may not wish to regard your sermon as ipso facto the Word of the Lord. There is wisdom in that; it's not a matter only of humility! But you also stand a fair chance of doing a disservice to the Word and to the hearers if you prepare and if you preach as though the people were not listening to hear the voice of the Lord through your sermon. It is perhaps a seeming contradiction that the voice of the Lord can be heard *in the response of another believer to that same voice.* But the mature faithful, at least, will have learned to listen at all times and in all places for that beloved and terrifying voice. If they do not hear it in the lesson and sermon, they have a right to feel disappointed.

But the preacher's posture of co-offerer of worship does not justify, let alone require, a separate "pulpit liturgy." Rereading of the lesson(s), collects and prayers, invocations, salutations, introductions, greetings, and other ritual embroidery, together with such ceremonial embellishments as have been known to evolve—fiddlings with lights, books, markers, clips, papers, pencils, glasses (tumblers or spectacles), handkerchiefs, watches, pills, and the paraphernalia of electronic public address—are all too often symptomatic of that sense of preachifying self-importance which (among other things) has done little for the good name and estate of the office! If you are up there to preach, do it; that is, do that, and not something else! The pulpit is not the place for a private mass; personal devotions are for "the closet," not for display.

There are in addition, of course, the continuing dialogues between preacher and individual listener, between preacher and congregation, and between congregation and individual. These dialogues may take several liturgical shapes, but all should be informed by the dialogical principle as laid out in chapter 10. The preacher whose work does justice to its liturgical context will be sensitive to all of these dimensions of dialogue and will shape his or her discourse accordingly. But one word needs to be said at this point in particular, although it could well open and close each chapter in any book on preaching: the primary reality, the most important transaction, the one conversation that must not be interrupted, diverted, or otherwise hindered, is that between the community of belief—as a whole and as individual members—on the one hand and, on the other, the Lord God who has promised, when two or three gather in his name, to be there. If the Lord is not there, if that dialogue is only theoretical or only "suggested by the human dialogue" (or some other euphemism for unreality), and if the preacher's behavior so implies, then both the worship and the preaching are sham, and the participants the victims of a pathetic delusion.[8] Notice the step which the preacher of "The Eye of the Storm" takes, right toward the close, to secure the acknowledgment of the Presence!

"Just as liturgical space—the naves, chancels, and altars which we set apart as holy—becomes the center of the universe to the bowing worshiper, so narrative can become a sacred time to which all our years and days are oriented" (Rice, above).

Let us observe that the transformation works both ways: one can begin, that is, with a narrative, a story, and find that as narrator and listener bend to each other under the "spell," or story, they have in effect entered into sacred time. Or one can begin, alternatively, with a sacralization of time, a hallowing and a way of consecrating periods of time whose development and refinement—and major configurations—are centuries old, and find that this sacred time constitutes and hallows and tells and preserves . . . a story. The sacred time, the sacred period of periods, is called the church year, and its story is precisely The Story of the mystery of the Word of God and of the mighty saving acts of God.[9]

So it is that the year of the church becomes in itself the *God-spell* and the raconteur par excellence of the mystery/story. It has been no small matter for the church to have, and repeatedly to rediscover, the structure and dynamic of the year. For how better, how more reliably, could the church be assured that when the story is told, it will be told right, and not, with its parts out of order and proportion, like a joke poorly told, sag or collapse of its own weight with a mangled punch line? How be better assured of the continued faithful patterning of the Christian life, of the congregational commitment, and of the preaching of the Word within this master plan of the Story of God, which plan persists and endures regardless of the careerings of the theologians, the hummings of parish programs (or the creaking or thundering of denominational or ecumenical programs), the vagaries of the psychic "market" in the pew, the digestions of the preachers, or the "passages" through which each or any may currently be moving!

For the preacher, of course, the year means basically the discipline of the lectionary. It is a stroke of great good fortune, at least, for preachers now beginning their work, that a new three-year lectionary has been developed and has already begun to enjoy wide approval and use in Roman Catholicism and in many major sectors of Protestant Christianity. Based essentially on the Roman *Ordo Lectionum Missae,* it takes advantage of the enormous advances of recent decades in biblical theology, it is responsive to liturgical research and renewal, it has been designed with an eye on social developments within Western culture and church life, it is attentive to and accurately reflective of the year of the church, of course, and—not the least of its numerous values—it has been constructed with preaching in mind. Preachers who are as yet unfamiliar with this lectionary would do well to become familiar with its rationale, its structure, its spirit, and its potential assistance in the telling of The Story by looking up the introduction to one or another of the denominational variations on the basic structure.[10]

Adherence to a lectionary will not, of course, guarantee that the resultant preaching will be biblical, evangelical, confessional, relevant, or anything else. Nor will adherence reduce even slightly the exegetical task. Nor will it disclose (as a quick inspection of the tables will make clear) any arcane harmonized system which guarantees some kind of unity among the lessons for any given Sunday. What adherence will provide is one more guide, one more instrument, to help the preacher and the people make sure that The Story is clearly and consistently told, and told right, across the year and the years.

Fidelity to the lectionary, it should perhaps be added, does not even assure that the preaching is liturgical, let alone biblical or evangelical. For there are uses of the lectionary itself which, liturgically speaking, are either merely insensitive or downright counterproductive. The preacher must decide, again and again, which lection(s) to use, what plan of expository attack to employ, what the thrust, bearing, and tone of the sermon shall be, what its language and illustration. The preacher must ask repeatedly what considerations should govern decisions to exploit the lectionary's openings into courses of sermons on particular portions of Scripture. There are, or should be, liturgical components of all such decisions, as well as pastoral, exegetical, social, and doctrinal considerations.

And of course there are uncomfortable texts. Nobody promised the preacher a rose garden.[11] (And besides, every Sunday has three lessons.) And although it is possible on a given Sunday to abandon the lectionary, for cause, for the text of the sermon, there is a great deal to be said for having addressed an issue on a scriptural base, as provided by the lectionary, in the recent past; that is, before the pressure of a sequence of events *forces* the preacher to address it, with or without the support of the lectionary.

There are good reasons from time to time to stray from the lectionary—but among those reasons should not be the unspoken assumption that the community of faith can come to grips with a question in the liturgy *only* if the preacher tackles it head-on in the sermon! There are among other things the prayers of the church, which, if homiletical only at peril of (at best) insolence, may often be the most responsible way of dealing with a new, hot question—perhaps especially if it is the kind which makes the preacher say—into the mirror on Saturday afternoon—"I *must* speak out!"

The lectionary is constructed chiefly in response to the year and in view of the whole counsel of Scripture. It is not constructed to deal in systematic terms with discrete questions of public policy or social justice. But the reasons for this include not least the conviction that the truth and power of the gospel are such as to create, when the Word is "rightly divided," a vision of justice and of peace which is derived from the vision and revelation of Almighty God—apart from which, for the believer, the passion for social justice can constitute only idolatry. The preacher and people who are responsibly attuned to the year and the lectionary will not need to "go further" than the lectionary except in times of true and emergent crisis.

This chapter has offered a basically liturgical view of preaching. That is to say, liturgy is worship; worship is essentially an act of adoration; the lesson is provided as an occasion of that act, and the sermon is provided, as it were, to assure that the worshiper hears, receives, the lesson. It should be clear that such preaching offers not only the clarity and power and depth, and the affirmation and integration, which might reasonably be expected from the proper doing of a piece of good liturgy, but as well, joy, surprise, remorse and penitence, awe, aspiration, exaltation. And it should be clear that liturgical preaching accomplishes this not despite but because of its liturgical integrity—that is to say, because those are appropriate responses to The Story in the text and to the one to whom the text bears witness: the Lamb of God and King of Kings.

NOTES

1. There are notable exceptions. One of them is Roy Pearson, *The Preacher: His Purpose and Practice* (Philadelphia: Westminster Press, 1962), chap. 7.

2. See Arthur C. Piepkorn in *The Liturgical Renewal of the Church*, ed. Massey H. Shepherd (New York: Oxford University Press, 1960), chap. 3.

3. For further elaboration see the major essay by Aidan Kavanagh in *The Roots of Ritual*, ed. James Shaughnessy (Grand Rapids: William B. Eerdmans Publishing Co., 1973).

4. Consider for example the implications for the church and for the doctrine of the ministry if the body—and life-style—of the preacher be regarded as one of the sacramental *materia* of the cult!

5. E. Shillito, in *Christian Worship: Studies in Its History and Meaning*, ed. Nathaniel Micklem (London: Oxford University Press, 1936), pp. 216–17.

6. See Paul F. Bosch, *Sermon as Part of Liturgy* (St. Louis: Concordia Publishing House, 1977), chap. 2; James T. Hall, "Measuring the Com-

munication of Feeling during Worship," *Pastoral Psychology* 14 (October 1963): 50-55; and Paul Harms, *Power from the Pulpit* (St. Louis: Concordia Publishing House, 1977), p. 37.

7. The question will surely be raised by future-minded readers whether the function of preaching must be understood in terms of the preacher's behavior. For reasons which are far too various and substantial to discuss here, the present writer believes that while there may be a place, from time to time, under certain special circumstances, for the use of liturgical dance or movies or "dialogue sermons" or chancel drama or "multimedia" presentations in the place of the sermon, the future of the office does not lie to any significant degree in that direction. There is however a provocative discussion of some of these matters in the book cited above by Paul Bosch, and there are some helpful observations by Edward Fischer in the Kavanagh symposium cited earlier.

8. For a further discussion of this question see Dietrich Ritschl, *Memory and Hope* (New York: Macmillan Publishing Co., 1967). Perhaps it should also be said just once, simply in order that it not remain unsaid: unless worship is understood not merely as fellowship, not merely as dialogue, but also and ultimately as participation in the cosmic and altogether secular project of almighty God for the redemption of a fallen world, it is just as surely so much wasted time, and little more than self-delusion.

9. See Louis Bouyer, *Life and Liturgy* (London: Sheed & Ward, 1956), pp. 185-86.

10. Especially helpful is *The Church Year Calendar and Lectionary,* Contemporary Worship 6 (Philadelphia: Board of Publication, Lutheran Church in America, 1973), pp. 3-46.

11. There are also those times when the lectionary provides a text which seems, perhaps more to the people than to the preacher, to be "a hard saying" in the context of the previous week. It is an enormous relief at such times to have had a good record of fidelity to the lectionary!

6

Preaching in
Pastoral Perspective

Norman Neaves

The telephone rang late one evening. A woman in our church had just found out that she had lost a hotly contested fight for the custody of her two children—and also that she would have to move from the family's home in less than a month so that her estranged husband and two boys could begin living there. Her feeling of despair was deep and poignant.

There were lots of needs that cried out for pastoral care, both on the telephone that night and also in more structured and intentional environments through the weeks that followed. But are those the only places and settings in which pastoral care can occur? Perhaps that woman would be at the service on Sunday morning. Could the pulpit too be a setting for pastoral care? And how about the gathered community, worshiping God and celebrating its common life, as an arena in which comfort and care are mediated?

Those questions spun in my mind as I drove to the office the next morning for a day of sermon preparation for Passion Sunday. And at the center of those questions were the needs of the young woman whose world had collapsed only a few hours before and who stood at the border of a deepening despair. What could I say, as one called to stand between the Word and the world, that would be significant to her? And given that the sermon dare not exploit her vulnerability nor betray her confidence nor make her feel acutely conspicuous and self-conscious, how could I possibly say something that would reach her in her acute but unique situation? A sense of balance would have to be struck between being so particular as to invade the privacy of a human being and being so general as to sound clichéd and essentially irrelevant. How could that balance be achieved?

Of course there was another option too, namely, to decline to deal with such matters in the pulpit, an option which essentially divorces the sermon from such intensely personal concerns. But I have been a pastor long enough to feel increasingly uncomfortable with this option. I'm tired of sermons that don't live where people live, that don't connect with the real stories and struggles by which their lives are shaped, that never touch the earth or breathe the air that the congregation breathes. Maybe there are those who enjoy developing the universal sermon, the one that can be preached everywhere and anywhere, that has a quality of being timeless. But as far as I am concerned, everywhere and anywhere really mean nowhere; and those who strive to be timeless are, usually, simply not very timely. Besides, I'm less interested in being the great pulpiteer who builds for himself a reputation than in being a parish pastor who builds with others a congregation. To me, Kierkegaard was right when he suggested that the particular is higher than the universal.[1] Let me be involved with the specific, and maybe somehow the cosmic will take care of itself.

I am one of those who have adopted the practice of writing every sermon with four or five people in mind, as was suggested in chapter 4. And on that particular Thursday morning, as I sat down at my desk to begin writing, I "invited" that young woman with whom I had talked the night before, and three or four others who had experienced similar tragedies, into the chamber of my personal reflections and thoughts. Although they never knew what an instrumental role they had played in the development of that sermon, actually they were the ones who created it with me. They peered over my shoulder, as it were, while I penciled my manuscript into being; and throughout the day we had numerous "conversations" with one another as I thought about sections of the sermon in light of who they are and where they are. I found myself "asking" them whether this thought or that idea was meaningful and whether it spoke to them at the points of their particular need, and more than once I found myself rewriting my manuscript or trying to say things just a little bit more simply because they "spoke back" to me and told me where they were. It was a far better sermon than it would have been if they had not cooperated.

Their collaboration does not need to be invisible. I block out at least fifteen hours a week for counseling sessions, some of them on a one-to-one basis and others with groups. A colleague of mine, in discovering that commitment, remarked that it seemed to him an inefficient use of time. He felt that much more could be accomplished if that time were spent on sermon preparation or on speeches to be given to certain large groups; it would cost fewer minutes per person. From my point of view, however, those counseling appointments are an integral and indispensable element in my sermon preparation. They provide the material against which I am able to hear and appropriate and understand the Word, the context out of which my preaching has a chance to be relevant and alive and responsive to human need; and if I had not spent considerable time in such appointments, I'm not sure I would have "heard" from anyone as I sat down to write my sermon that Thursday morning—or any other Thursday morning, for that matter. The sermon is not an exposition of the Word alone but an exposition of the Word in the context of the world. And whenever the sermon fails to stand between the Word and the world, keeping both in balanced perspective, it cannot be a real "Word-event," as Ernst Fuchs is so fond of putting it.[2] This is to say, then, that my counseling is done both from the perspective of pastoral care and from the perspective of preaching, and that neither can be separated from the other without great impairment of both.

Let's return to the woman who called that night, and to the problem which distress like hers can create for a preacher. How can one preach in a way that addresses the real needs of people without exploiting their vulnerability or betraying their confidence or making them feel acutely conspicuous and self-conscious? In short, how can the preacher avoid being a tattletale in the pulpit and yet still be relevant to the real issues in the lives of individual men and women? The answer lies in the use of the human stories that make up novels, plays, television dramas, movies, and comedy routines. These stories are relevant and marketable precisely because they grow out of the real life stories of actual human beings. That's why they touch us in such sensitive and emotional ways. That's why we cry or laugh or feel deeply moved and maybe inspired, or sense ourselves becoming profoundly quieted and stilled upon encountering such stories—whether in print or on screen or on a stage. They are, finally, *our* stories and the stories of those to whom we preach. And therefore, as we find ways to utilize these stories in our sermons, we will be addressing the deeply personal issues in the lives of our members—those issues that emerge out of the pastoral caring that we share—without violating confidences, exploiting vulnerabilities, or misusing a sacred trust that has been placed in our care. It's as if those stories function as a homiletical Rorschach into which people can read their own dramas as well as their own subjective meanings.

The particular story that came to my mind as I wrestled with that woman's dilemma was the experience of despair that Sam Keen describes in the opening lines of his book *Beginning Without End:*

> Nearing the mythical age of forty I fell in love with a young woman, and left a home that had been rich in care, in fighting, in lovemaking on Sunday mornings, in shared memories of the birth of children, in the myriad details that weave the lives of solitary individuals into a single family. Whether divorce was an act of courage or betrayal remains moot. Beyond question I found myself at mid-life in a radical crisis; like a plant whose roots had been torn from accustomed soil. One rainy morning I awoke alone in an apartment in San Francisco with the realization that my marriage had finished, my wife had remarried, my children were living far away, my lover had departed, and my academic career had been abandoned. My emotional capital seemed exhausted. My past looked infinitely richer than any future I might create. Depression lurked and easily invaded any empty moment. I had either to surrender to despair or mourn the death of my old life and find some way to begin again.[3]

What a story! And what a vivid description of that young woman's feeling! Sam Keen went through a period of his life just like the one she was going through—a period of wrenching personal bankruptcy and almost total despair—and in sharing that experience out of his story, I did, in effect, touch upon that experience in her story—and no telling how many similar stories in the lives of others. It's as if what is most true in the experience of one person is bound also to be true, to some degree, of the experience of every person, as was suggested in chapter 4.

Sam Keen's experience was not a literary experience, but I became familiar with it in the course of my reading. I have always enjoyed reading, but never in my life have I done as much reading as I have *had* to do since becoming a parish minister. It is a major priority in the budgeting of my time each week, because it supplies me with the images and stories which I need if I am to deal with deeply personal issues. Moreover, the character of my reading has changed substantially since those days immediately following seminary. I used to spend most of my time reading systematic theologies (my field of major concentration in seminary) and poring over exegetical studies. It put me in touch with the Word *conceptually,* but not with the Word *contextually.* Increasingly, however, I find that the bulk of my reading centers more and more in novels, plays, short stories, articles, and biographies, and I have become much more discriminating in watching television and movies. It's not that I'm no longer interested in systematic theology and biblical exegesis. I am quite interested in both and spend significant portions of time in each. But neither has much meaning for me anymore apart from the life issues which real human beings are encountering.

The Old Testament text appointed for Passion Sunday, for example, was the story of the valley of dry bones in Ezekiel 37. What a correlation there is between the question posed in that passage ("Can these bones live again?"), the decision Sam Keen confronted ("to surrender to despair or mourn the death of my old life and find some way to begin again"), and the fundamental issue with which that woman was struggling when she called me on the telephone that night and poured out her despair! I entitled my sermon "Beginning with an Ending," and I felt it was faithful to the theme of Ezekiel 37, reflective of the struggle which Sam Keen had faced, and responsive to the life situation of that woman. My thesis was, "Existence is that which moves from a beginning to an ending, but life is that which moves from an ending to a beginning."

I am convinced, in other words, that preaching both can and must emerge out of one's pastoral caring.

The issue that presented me with the greatest difficulty upon getting out of seminary and beginning to develop as a preacher was the whole issue of being prophetic in the pulpit. And I think the difficulty lay in two essentially interrelated concerns: first, how one could be prophetic without alienating a congregation; and second, how one could be prophetic without impairing one's role in pastoral care. In other words, is it possible for one to be a pastor and a prophet at the same time? Can one stand "over against" a congregation in the tradition of a prophet and proclaim the unequivocal "Thus saith the Lord" while at the same time being identified with the congregation in the tradition of a priest and mediating the comfort of grace? It seemed to me an either-or issue, one that was basically irreconcilable.

I soon began to see that the crux of my dilemma lay largely at the point of what it meant to be prophetic. The predominant image in my mind was that of distance and austerity, a stance which reflects a state of alienation and that tends to produce an even greater alienation. I thought of a prophet as one who hassled and harangued others, a person who came from "God's side" of things with a pompous and pontificating Word rather than a person who stood on the "human side" of things and shared the dilemma of the people with them. And that image, accurate or not, was the one that created my conflict between being a pastor on the one hand and a prophet on the other.

I suppose there's a place for the evangelist who comes into a church or a community and creates a lot of excitement about the Christian gospel, but I've often wondered how much excitement or enthusiasm he could maintain if he didn't leave in two weeks but had to face the challenge of living out the gospel with a particular group of people over a period of years. Undoubtedly the shape of his evangelism would change if he were not afforded the luxury of being a hit-and-run preacher—and maybe also the tone of his zeal, too.

Likewise, I suppose there's a place for the prophetic voice that speaks to the church or to a community from outside of its life—the voice that sharply states the idealisms of the gospel and that rings boldly with strong moral imperatives and that engenders a sense of guilt in the consciences of its hearers—but as with the evangelist, I've often wondered how strongly stated would be her maxims if she too weren't a hit-and-run preacher who didn't face the challenge of being *with* people over a great period of their lives.

I certainly do not mean to imply that there's no place for either the work of the evangelist or the work of the prophet as I've just presented them here. We can be grateful that there are such people and that their gifts can be appropriated on behalf of the church, both locally and globally. But for the parish minister to preach evangelistically or prophetically in the style of either, or to understand his function as that of an evangelist or prophet on the model of either, is to make a serious mistake. If parish preaching is to be effective, the preacher must be an evangelist of a different sort and must preach prophetically in another way.

I have come to feel that my own prophetic preaching must grow out of my own identification with the people with whom I am the church. I am less and less interested in preaching *to* them about the great moral issues of the day than I am in struggling *with* them through the complex dilemmas in which we find ourselves. My own participation in "the sin of the world" is no longer as hidden from me as it was in the early days of my ministry, and with that growing realization has come a greater sense of humility in how I preach and handle the prophetic Word. It's as a man in our church once expressed it: "When you point a finger at someone, remember that there are three fingers pointing back at you!" I remember that more readily these days.

I remember also a remark that Arthur Schlesinger once made as he was analyzing a complex set of international issues. He said: "There are no simple solutions to the world's problems. We must be delivered from the great simplifiers these days who fail to realize the utter complexity of modern life." There is a place for moral leadership, to be sure, and certainly no responsible person can afford duck a clear moral issue. But the sheer complexity of life today requires that moral leadership be exercised less presumptuously than before. Surely its tone should convey no naive certainty but must bespeak the struggle, the reflection, and the deep grappling for which the webbings of complexity clearly call. And are not most matters caught in those kinds of webbings these days?

I have sometimes found that a sermon which raises the questions in a thoughtful and profound way is actually more prophetic today than a sermon which makes bold and exclamatory statements from beginning to end. That's not to say there's no place for the exclamation mark in a responsibly prophetic sermon. But it is to suggest that the searching question searchingly posed may have more power to awaken the contemporary conscience than any other means at our disposal as preachers.

Let me share one of my own struggles of a couple of years ago, a struggle out of which I preached a series of prophetic sermons. A member of our congregation is the executive director of the Oklahoma County libraries. He found himself embroiled in a major public controversy at that time concerning the availability of "sex books" on the shelves of the various branches of the library system. These were books written for teenage boys and girls just about to enter puberty, and were designed to provide them with accurate information about their own emerging sexuality. They were written, moreover, by a past president of the American Psychological Association, and were endorsed by that body as well.

The controversy developed because a certain county commissioner decided to make an issue of the availability of these books; he declared them pornographic and demanded either that they be removed from the shelves immediately or that the director be ousted from his position. The net effect of his remarks was to touch off a prairie fire of emotionalism throughout this part of the Bible belt, and soon it was surging so widely that one wondered if it could ever be brought under control again. Fundamentalist Christians began rising up everywhere, demanding the removal of both the books and the director, and over four hundred ministers in the metropolitan area signed a petition to the same effect, calling for a return to "common decency and to the old-fashioned values that gave birth to this republic." Not one of the clergy dared to speak out on the other side of the issue, even so remotely as to suggest that maybe, just maybe, there might be a certain compatibility between those "sex books" and the basic ethic of the Christian faith.

I decided to be that person—not simply because the director is a member of our congregation, but also because the Christian faith is often entrapped and ensnarled in a kind of puritanism that just isn't faithful to the gospel, at least as I understand it. Someone was needed to speak out on behalf of the kind of incarnationalism that stands at the heart of the Christian message, and that affirms rather than denies the essential wholeness of personhood—an incarnationalism which not only embraces human sexuality but which approaches it openly rather than obliquely. The matter wasn't as easily resolved as that, of course; underlying it were such other concerns as censorship and civil rights, the relationship between freedom and responsibility, the problem of pluralism in the establishment of social values, the nature of the democratic process, and the protection of minority rights, to mention a few! Moreover, I began asking myself some more professional and personal questions too: Is there a difference between censorship in this particular instance and the kind of "censorship" that is exercised by the Federal Communications Commission in setting standards for national television programming? What right do I have to support the availability of these "sex books" because they do not offend my set of social values when I am not willing to extend that support into the area of child pornography, which greatly offends my social values? In other words, who am I to draw the line? If the Christian faith is called to influence the quality of human life, how sharply critical can I afford to be of those others who also seek to influence that quality out of the same Christian faith, even though both their standards and their methods may differ from mine?

To sum up, what began in my soul as a strongly felt prophetic issue was tempered somewhat when I allowed its initial simplicities to be seen in the wider context of its complexities. Although I nevertheless preached out of my initial conviction and bias, I did so with much more humility and tentativeness than I would have in the beginning. Rather than making strongly assertive statements and smugly feeling that I was being prophetic, I made much more thoughtful statements that involved the congregation in the overall dilemma. I tried to give my "prophecy" a probing, questioning inflection rather than a dogmatic or authoritarian tone. Maybe, to say it differently, prophetic preaching can be done much more effectively with some carefully chosen question marks rather than with a whole bunch of big exclamation marks. In fact, maybe prophetic preaching is that which addresses and struggles with and lives the great questions of life with a group of people who are called the church—the kind of prophetic preaching that Jesus did with the woman at the well when his probing questions helped center her in the deeper concerns of her life.

Perhaps Rilke has expressed it as well as anyone in his *Letters to a Young Poet*. At one point he says, "Be patient toward all that is unsolved in your heart. And try to love the questions themselves. Do not seek the answers that cannot be given you because you would not be able to live them. And the point is to live everything. Live the questions now. Perhaps you will then gradually, without noticing it, live along some distant day into the answer."[4]

Living the questions, *really* living them in all of their complexity and intensity, may be at the heart of the meaning of the prophetic in our time. At least, that's the way I'm expressing it at this point in my life.

If you were to visit our church's building and take a look at the room in which we worship, one of the things that would surely catch your attention would be the portability of all the pieces of furniture throughout the space. Not only are the chairs portable, but also the baptismal font which is usually located at one end of the room, and the twenty-foot communion table which is positioned in the center. Moreover, not only are the risers upon which the choir sits portable, but so is the pulpit from which I preach Sunday after Sunday.

One day I was watching our janitor disassemble the room from a distance, and as he rolled out the big communion table and then muscled the four-hundred-pound pulpit onto a dolly, I couldn't help being struck once again by the contrast of events that take place in that space. Only an hour or so before, we had completed the second of our two worship services for the day. In another hour and a half, a community-wide political forum featuring the state gubernatorial candidates would be under way in the same place. And then later that night, following one of their meetings, a group of teenagers would be setting up a volleyball net in the room and vigorously engaging themselves in some spirited games before finally saying good night to the place and going home. It's hard to think of that room as a sanctuary in the more popular sense of that word, and it's hard to think of preaching in that room without somehow relating the sermon to the other events which happen there.

The program of our church is quite extensive and offers a variety of opportunities for persons within our church family and also within the larger metropolitan area. It includes political forums featuring mayoral candidates and gubernatorial candidates and school-board candidates as well as special courses in auto mechanics and macrame and disco dancing. It includes seminars in creative writing and photography and natural childbirth as well as discussion groups on parenting and time management and modern existentialism. It includes programs on death and dying and energy alternatives and prison reform as well as instruction in tennis and golf and backpacking and organic gardening. It includes the sponsorship of two preschools, one

housed in our own building and the other in an inner-city neighbor-
hood, as well as the operation of an arts and crafts shop, also housed
in our own building, which generates income for additional mission
involvements in our metropolitan area. And it includes many, many
more programs and events—usually forty-five to fifty each spring and
each fall. The point is that these programs and events are a natural
consequence of the preaching themes that have been developed over
the last ten years.

I do not wish to imply that I am some kind of pulpit giant whose
preaching has produced a phenomenal church. Far from it! But it is
clear to me that the relationship between preaching and program in
my own case is certainly applicable to that relationship in the case of
other pastors too—and it is in this awareness that I share my own
reflections and observations. My sharings have to do with the place of
theology in one's preaching, and more specifically with the way in
which preaching bridges the gap between theology on the one hand
and church development on the other.

As I see it, it is impossible to divorce preaching from theology (for
that matter, it is also impossible to divorce theology from preaching),
and the central theological theme that has influenced my own
preaching most heavily can be stated concisely in the words of
Irenaeus in the second century: "The glory of God is man fully alive."
In my opinion, the central purpose of the church is to enable human
life to become more fully human. The church exists to enable human
beings, both collectively and individually, to experience a sense of
wholeness and fullness and to grow into their potential as persons. The
church is not primarily to relate persons to God so much as to help
persons realize that God is the one who chooses to be related to us. Or
to say it differently, the church is centered not so much in the worship
of God as in the celebration of God's Word; the Word proclaims not
only our acceptability before him but also the possibility of our
becoming whole and responsive human beings. As Louis Evely, the
Catholic theologian, put it in his book *Our Prayer*: "It is pretty
shocking to discover after years of Christian education that there is no
such thing as the worship of God in Christianity. Christ did not come
to be served; he came to serve."[5]

Now it is not my purpose in this context to argue the merits of my
own persuasion, nor to elaborate on its thesis any more fully. I present

its essence only in order to demonstrate how one's theological formulation is integral to one's preaching and also how the content of one's preaching eventuates in the shape and style of a congregation's life. I have discovered that effective preaching begins not with technique and methodology but rather with a pressing conviction about the essential meaning of the gospel. And I have also discovered that effective preaching depends much less upon personal charisma or engaging oratory than upon a consistent perspective and a thoroughly digested theology.

The really crucial thing for me, as I look back upon ten years of preaching in the same congregational community, is not any one sermon in particular, or any four or five sermons that were especially pivotal, so much as the cumulative effect of all the sermons put together. The issue ultimately rests with the basic theological principle that has undergirded all of the various accents of the liturgical year. And if that theological principle had not been clearly formulated in my own mind and deeply rooted in my own personal convictions, I do not see how my preaching could have had any bearing upon the shape and style of our congregation's life.

I don't want to be misunderstood at this point. I suffer from no delusions of grandeur that my sermons have had a direct bearing upon the kinds of programs that have developed in our church and that somehow a particular sermon or two brought into being a particular course or direction. What I believe, however, is that my sermons have helped to establish a theological milieu, a sensitivity to the possibility of certain activities derived from faithful membership thoughtfully considered. That milieu and sensitivity have evoked all kinds of creative expressions and all kinds of innovative programs. I don't think we can escape the fact, in other words, that the pulpit sets the stage and the tone of a congregation's life and that invariably the strength of a congregation is somehow proportional to the strength of its preaching over a period of years.

There's one more thing that I want to say about my preaching in relationship to our church's programming: the relationship has been a two-way street. Not only has my preaching had a bearing upon our church's programming, but our church's programming has had a bearing upon my preaching too. I have seen the gospel enacted before my eyes time and time again as I have watched people grow and develop through involvements in our church's community. I have seen the parables of Jesus enacted before my eyes in the human dramas that have unfolded in our midst. I have watched Israel grapple with the great ethical concerns of life in the public forums and political debates and timely seminars that are constantly being developed in our community's life. And through it all I have had a feeling of standing in the same place where Amos stood, of catching a glimpse of the same visions that inspired Isaiah and Jeremiah, and of coming up against the same stuff and the same eventfulness that Peter experienced and that Paul knew and that finally gave rise to the early Christian community. I have come to see, in other words, that the eventfulness that gave birth to the church two thousand years ago is the same eventfulness that continues to give birth to our church even today; and that precisely the kinds of envisionings that brought the people of Israel into being are the envisionings that also bring us into being.

Do you remember how Jesus put it when John the Baptist's friends asked if he were the Messiah? He said, "Go and tell John what you have seen and heard: the blind receive their sight, the lame walk, lepers are cleansed, and the deaf hear, the dead are raised up, the poor have good news preached to them." Through the programs of our church I have seen "the blind receive their sight" and "the lame walk." Through the programs of our church I have seen "lepers" cleansed and the "dead" raised to newness of life. And through the programs of our church I have seen "deaf" people begin to "hear" for the first time and the "poor" receive the Word of their liberation and their promise.

What I'm saying is that the church has become a truly eschatological community for me over the past ten years—a community in which eschaton has been glimpsed, tasted, and in which the presence of the kingdom has been experienced at first hand. And since I have been an eyewitness to these "mighty acts of the Lord," I have felt myself empowered and inspired in ways I had never experienced before. Paul is no longer simply a historical figure whose Epistles I read in the New Testament but several different persons in our own community of faith with whom I talk almost daily. Jesus is not merely a man about whom I read in the Gospels but one who appears and reappears in the flesh of many with whom I am privileged to live. And the prophets are not just ancient people who spoke courageously in the long ago but men and women whom I see speaking forcibly at an energy seminar or debating articulately in a political forum or pushing intently for a piece of legislation at a statewide rally for prison reform. They are all persons in my midst whose stories weave once again the threads of The Story and who share with me the gifts of grace that enable renewed preaching to occur.

Every church has its own unique setting and its own unique story. It is an eschatological community in which the kingdom of God is forever appearing, however obliquely, and in which "the mighty acts of the Lord" are taking place daily. And it occurs to me that the task of the pastor is to see those acts with the eyes of faith when they happen and to realize that one's preaching is rooted in them every bit as much as it's rooted in the historic acts of long ago.

Our theology is not so much what we bring to our context as it is a response to what happens in our context, a response that helps us in our preaching to clarify what is happening among us.

To say it again, then: preaching is a two-way street. It brings the church into being and it is also brought into being by the church. It produces the shape and form of a congregation's life, and yet it is shaped and formed by that congregation's life. It is the medium through which the Word gives meaning to the world and also the medium through which the world gives meaning to the Word. As I see it, preaching always takes place between those two polarities, and the program of the church is that point where they most clearly come into focus.

NOTES

1. Sören Kierkegaard, "Fear and Trembling," in *A Kierkegaard Anthology,* ed. Robert Breatall (New York: Random House, The Modern Library, 1946), pp. 116–34.

2. Ernst Fuchs, "Proclamation and Speech Event," *Theology Today* 21 (October 1964): 348.

3. Sam Keen, *Beginnings Without End* (New York: Harper & Row, Publishers, 1975), p. ix.

4. Rainer Maria Rilke, *Letters to a Young Poet* (New York: W. W. Norton & Co., 1934).

5. Louis Evely, *Our Prayer* (New York: Herder & Herder, 1970), p. 26.

SERMON:

The Eye of the Storm

Edmund A. Steimle

In those days a decree went out from Caesar Augustus that all the world should be enrolled. This was the first enrollment, when Quirinius was governor of Syria. And all went to be enrolled, each to his own city. And Joseph also went up from Galilee, from the city of Nazareth, to Judea, to the city of David, which is called Bethlehem, because he was of the house and lineage of David, to be enrolled with Mary, his betrothed, who was with child. And while they were there, the time came for her to be delivered. And she gave birth to her firstborn son and wrapped him in swaddling cloths, and laid him in a manger, because there was no place for them in the inn.

And in that region there were shepherds out in the field, keeping watch over their flock by night. And an angel of the Lord appeared to them, and the glory of the Lord shone around them, and they were filled with fear. And the angel said to them, "Be not afraid; for behold, I bring you good news of a great joy which will come to all the people; for to you is born this day in the city of David a Savior, who is Christ the Lord. And this will be a sign for you: you will find a babe wrapped in swaddling cloths and lying in a manger." And suddenly there was with the angel a multitude of the heavenly host praising God and saying,

"Glory to God in the highest,
and on earth peace among men with whom he is pleased!"

When the angels went away from them into heaven, the shepherds said to one another, "Let us go over to Bethlehem and see this thing that has happened, which the Lord has made known to us." And they went with haste, and found Mary and Joseph, and the babe lying in a manger. And when they saw it they made known the saying which had been told them concerning this child; and all who heard it wondered at what the shepherds told them. But Mary kept all these things, pondering them in her heart. And the shepherds returned, glorifying and praising God for all they had heard and seen, as it had been told them.

Luke 2:1–20

I think I shall never forget the time when hurricane Hazel, back in the fifties, was sweeping through eastern Pennsylvania and hit Philadelphia, where we were living at the time, head on. Unlike most hurricanes, which lose much of their force when they turn inland, this one hit with all the fury of a hurricane at sea: drenching rains, screaming winds, trees uprooted, branches flying through the air, broken power lines crackling on the pavements. It was frightening. Then suddenly there was a letup, a lull. Shortly all was still. Not a leaf quivered. The sun even broke through briefly. It was the eye of the storm. "All was calm, all was bright." And then all hell broke loose again: branches and trees crashing down, the screaming winds, the torrential rain, the power lines throwing out sparks on the pavement. But that was a breathless moment—when we experienced the eye of the storm.

Christmas Eve is something like that, like the experience of the eye of the storm. At least the first Christmas night. So Luke reports: "And she gave birth to her first-born son and wrapped him in swaddling cloths, and laid him in a manger, because there was no place for them in the inn." The Christmas crèche and the Christmas pageantry picture it so today: "All was calm, all was bright."

Mary . . . resting now, after the pain of the contractions and the delivery without benefit of anesthetic.

The child . . . sleeping peacefully in the swaddling cloths and the straw. At least we like to think him so. "Silent night, holy night." Of course, maybe his face was all contorted reds and purples with the frantic bleating of a newborn child, fists clenched, striking out at this new and strange environment after nine months in the warmth and security of the womb. But no. Let's picture him sleeping, exhausted perhaps from his frantic protests. "All is calm, all is bright. . . . Silent night, holy night." The eye of the storm.

For make no mistake, he comes at the center of a storm—both before and after the birth. The storm before: From devastation of a flood expressing the anger of God with a people whose every thought and imagination was evil, to his anger at the golden calf, to the destruction of Jerusalem and the Exile in Babylon, to Jonah desperately trying to run away from this God, to the narrow legalism of the Pharisees, to the oppression of the Roman occupation. He comes at the eye of the storm before.

And what followed this "silent night, holy night"? The storm after: The massacre of the innocent male children two years old and under by Herod in his frantic effort to deal with the threat of this child sleeping in the manger. And as he grew up, his family thought him a little bit nuts, his hometown neighbors threw him out of the synagogue when first he tried to preach. Then the sinister plots to do away with him, the angry mob crying for his blood on that first Good Friday, and the end? Death to the child.

What we tend to forget on Christmas is that these lovely stories of the birth—the manger, the shepherds, the angel chorus in the night sky, the wise men following the star and presenting their rare and expensive gifts—are not children's stories. If you think it takes children to make a Christmas, then you don't belong in church tonight. These are adult stories for adult Christians. Oh, let the children delight in them of course—and get out of them what they may. But they were written down by adult members of the early Christian community for other adult members of the Christian community.

Moreover, they are postresurrection stories, that is, they grew up in the tradition after the resurrection. Who knows where they came from? They came into being in the years following the resurrection as Negro spirituals came into being, as mature Christians pondered the mystery of the beginnings of this life whom they had seen die and rise again from the dead. They knew about the storm which preceded the birth. And they knew even more—first hand—about the storm that followed. They were not carried away by "the romantic fantasies of infancy." Like one standing in the eye of a hurricane, they were aware of the storm that went before and that followed.

And so tonight you and I come here, not wanting, I hope, to block out or forget the storms around us. Because if we do, we miss the whole point. We too are aware tonight of the storms which surround this "silent night, holy night."

We are aware of the confusion and destruction around us in the world. The violence in the Middle East, southern Africa, and Northern Ireland, the hunger in the Third World. Or closer to home, the muggings on the streets, the unemployment (a grim and passive kind of violence), the ghettos, the injustice to the blacks, the inner cities gutted by poverty and inflation and the massive indifference—sloth is the old-fashioned word for it—on the part of so many of us who do not live in the gutted inner cities. Moreover, we are aware of the precarious future which haunts all of us. People are dying this Christmas night as people die on every night. As one day, one night, you will die and I will die. And before that the inner loneliness which no one of us can entirely shake, and the specter of hopelessness which haunts us—for peace in the world, for the end of inflation, for families breaking up, for our nations as they drift along often so aimlessly, and for ourselves and our future.

The point is, we don't forget all this on Christmas Eve—or block it out. Like a person standing in the eye of a hurricane, we are aware of it all. If you want to forget it all tonight—OK! Go home and listen to Bing Crosby dreaming of a white Christmas. And there's a place for that—but not here!

For what other message on Christmas Eve is worth listening to? What peace? What hope? If it is simply a forgetting—when we can't forget, really—then we're reducing the Christmas story to a bit of nostalgia and indulging ourselves in the sentimental orgy which Christmas has become for so many, or we are reduced to the deep depression which grips so many others on Christmas Eve.

No. The Bible—praise God—tells it like it is. They saw the birth of the child as the eye of the storm—a peace which passes all understanding because it is not a peace apart from conflict, pain, suffering, violence, and confusion; that's the kind of peace we can understand all too well. But it's a peace like the peace in the eye of a hurricane, a peace smack in the middle of it all, a peace which indeed passes all understanding.

So in this hour, this night, worshiping at the manger of the child when "all is calm, all is bright," we rejoice in the hope born of the conviction that the storm, the destruction, the violence, the hopelessness, does not have the last word. But God—who gives us this "silent night" in the middle of the storm—he has the last word.

So rejoice . . . and sing the carols . . . and listen to the lovely ancient story and light the candles . . . and be glad—with your families, your friends, with the God who is above all and through all and in you all, who comes to us miraculously in this child, this night, when "all is calm, all is bright."

PART FOUR

THE MESSAGE

7

The Story of Good and Evil

Edmund A. Steimle

Amos Wilder has written, "Perhaps the special character of the [biblical] stories lies in the fact that they are not told for themselves, that they are not only about other people, but that they are always about us. They locate us in the very midst of the great story and plot of all time and space, and therefore relate us to the great dramatist and storyteller, God himself."[1]

Here, for example, is B. Davie Napier telling the story of Cain so that it becomes our story. It is Cain who is speaking, but it is of course me and my story being laid bare through the mouth of Cain:

> I hate his guts, I hate the guts of Abel.
> I'm sick of Abel, sick to death of Abel.
> Sick of brothers sick of fellows
> Blacks and Whites and Browns and Yellows
> Sick of Negro sick of Jew
> pressing pressing for his due
> sick of white men bastard white men
> arrogant and always right men
> sick of sick men sick of sickness
> Protestant- and Catholic-ness
> sick of every lying bromide
> Happy birthday Merry Yuletide
> Freedom truth and brotherhood
> Reader's Digest motherhood
> pledge allegiance to the flag
> "under God"—now what's the gag?
> Sick of vicious ostentation

sick of humor's constipation
sick of sickness human sickness
human greed and human thickness.
Get my brother off my back
White and Yellow Brown and Black.
Perish Abel perish quick—
One of us is awful sick.[2]

Now that rebellious outburst on the lips of Cain, which becomes through the preacher's sensitivity the same outburst on my own lips, brings us quite obviously to the problem of good and evil in relation to the biblical story. Actually, of course, the reason for the biblical story in the first place is the conflict between good and evil, the conflict between God's good will of love for humanity and humanity's refusal to live in accordance with God's good will. The early stories in Genesis make this clear. The creation story ends with "and God saw that it was good." And then the trouble begins with the story of Adam and Eve and the serpent in the garden, followed by the story of Cain and Abel, with Cain murdering his brother. Things go from bad to worse, and finally "the Lord saw that the wickedness of man was great on the earth, and that every imagination of the thoughts of his heart was only evil continually. And the Lord was sorry that he had made man on the earth, and it grieved him to his heart" (Gen. 6:5-6). Then follows the story of the flood, with God choosing the righteous Noah as a kind of second Adam to start the story all over again. But that doesn't work very well either, with the righteous Noah ending up in a drunken stupor.

So the story begins with the conflict between good and evil, between God's good will and humanity's refusal to accept and live by that will. But the biblical story is not of much help in explaining the why of evil in a world which God created good. The origin of evil is left ambiguous and mysterious. The biblical story is concerned more with the reality of evil and God's way of dealing with it than it is with any philosophical or theological or psychological explanation of the origin of evil. The existence of Satan is presupposed in the later writings, and the story of a fallen angel accounting for Satan doesn't help much in explaining the why of evil.

The most satisfying answer to the problem which I have come across comes from Reinhold Niebuhr's *The Nature and Destiny of*

Man.[3] Human beings, by virtue of the fact that they are mortal creatures who know that they are mortal creatures, are anxious, because
they cannot control their futures. Each knows that death will come,
and each is anxious. Anxiety also arises from the fact that human
beings know that there is much they do not know and never will
know—that too is out of control. And therefore each human being
feels that kind of anxiety too. This creaturely anxiety, caused by the
knowledge of ignorance and by the inevitability of death, both of
which mean the loss of control over one's future, one's destiny, is
neither good nor evil. It is a given. "Anxiety," according to Niebuhr,
"is the internal precondition of sin." In that creaturely anxiety a
human being has two choices: to say either "I trust God and his will
for me, and I trust him with my future too," or "To hell with that; by
God, I'll take my own future, my own destiny, into my own two hands
and work it out for myself." The early stories in Genesis: of Adam
and Eve in the garden, of Cain and Abel, of Noah, of the Tower of
Babel, simply illustrate how this initial rebellion issues in pride, lust,
gluttony, murder, apathy, selfishness, greed, injustice, and all the rest
of the evils which clutter up the landscapes of our lives. Evil, at its
root in the biblical story, is simply the refusal to trust God and his will
for us and for our future. Which is why faith is so prominent in the
story: it is the precondition of love.

The rest of the biblical story is a long account of how God deals
with this problem. His basic strategy is to evoke a person's freedom to
choose. A large part of his love for us is this respect for our freedom.
We are created "in his image," which means that we are created
capable of response to the God who made us. He will not bully or
coerce. His judgment on our rebelliousness is, for the most part,
simply to let the chips fall where they may. Meanwhile he chooses a
people who will multiply and be a blessing to all the nations of the
earth, and the blessing is that through the lives and witness of this
people to his faithfulness, his trustworthiness, they shall be a "light to
the Gentiles," evoking faith in God and his will.

So the stories of Abraham, of Moses and the liberation of the slaves
in Egypt, the passing through the Sea of Reeds, the stories of David,
of the prophets, right on through to the Christ story, are the working
out of this basic strategy to evoke faith in God and his will and thus to
"save" the people from their sins. "Repent and believe in the Lord

Jesus Christ" means essentially "In your anxiety as a creature, turn from taking matters into your own hands and trust the God who reveals his trustworthiness in Christ and in his love for you."

It is evident in the biblical story that evil appears not simply in personal or individual terms. It is also social. It infects the structures of society. As in a community we gather strength and courage and hope from others, so also do we encourage selfishness and pride and violence and lust in each other, and excuse and justify one another when we resort to selfishness and pride and violence and lust. The prophets, therefore, speak God's judgment not only upon individual and personal evils but also upon the evils of the church and the state. So Amos: "I hate, I despise your feasts, and I take no delight in your solemn assemblies. Even though you offer me your burnt offerings and cereal offerings, I will not accept them, and the peace offerings of your fatted beasts I will not look upon. Take away from me the noise of your songs; to the melody of your harps I will not listen. But let justice roll down like waters, and righteousness like an ever-flowing stream" (Amos 5:21-24). Nor is the judgment in Amos limited to the chosen people of Israel: "Thus says the Lord: 'For three transgressions of Damascus, and for four, I will not revoke the punishment . . . and the people of Syria shall go into exile to Kir,' says the Lord" (Amos 1:3-5).

But the biblical story, even as it is carried along through the prophets, is not basically or primarily a story of judgment. It is a story of God's grace, of his faithfulness, of his trustworthiness. For his strategy, even though it includes judgment, does not change. His strategy is to evoke faith, trust, and thus obedience to his will. So he offers visions of the future which illustrate his faithfulness. So in Micah: "He shall judge between many peoples, and shall decide for strong nations afar off; and they shall beat their swords into plowshares, and their spears into pruning hooks; nation shall not lift up sword against nation, neither shall they learn war anymore; but they shall sit every man under his vine and under his fig tree, and none shall make them afraid; for the mouth of the Lord of hosts has spoken" (Mic. 4:3-4).

So too to the people of Israel under the judgment of exile in Babylon the unknown prophet of the Exile speaks: "How beautiful upon the mountains are the feet of him who brings good tidings, who publishes peace, who brings good tidings of good, who publishes salvation, who says to Zion, 'Your God reigns.' . . . The Lord has bared His holy arm before the eyes of all the nations; and all the ends of the earth shall see the salvation of our God" (Isa. 52:7-10).

Despite the judgment leveled at hypocrisy in worship, at injustice and idolatry, the story is a story of God's faithful love for his people. He does not give up on them. The promise offered after the flood in the form of a rainbow is kept. His strategy for overcoming evil with good is to evoke faith and trust from the people, overcoming their anxiety, out of which evil springs, with the assurance of his love and his promises for the future.

Nowhere does this strategy for dealing with evil come through more plainly than in the Christ story. Here God himself enters into human history in the Christ figure, places himself at our disposal, makes himself vulnerable to all the evil in the world—for love is supremely expressed in vulnerability—even to evil's supreme expression, death.

Paul, in the second chapter of his Letter to the Philippians, celebrates the work of Christ in humility: ". . . who, though he was in the form of God, did not count equality with God a thing to be grasped, but emptied himself, taking the form of a servant, being born in the likeness of men. And being found in human form he humbled himself and became obedient unto death, even death on a cross" (Phil. 2:6-8). Here is the very opposite of the early stories in Genesis where people continually attempted to "count equality with God a thing to be grasped." But the Christ figure is content to live with his anxiety as a mortal creature who knows that he is a mortal creature and to trust God and thus to be obedient, even if it means death and darkness. "Have this mind in you . . ." says Paul.

Thus Christ becomes an example of the good, trusting, and obedient life for us: "Have this mind in you . . ." But if that were *all,* we would be of all people most miserable. For to hold Christ up as an example for me judges and condemns me and offers me no hope at all. I cannot possibly have the "mind of Christ" in me. But fortunately, that is *not* all. For God vindicates this trusting and obedient child of his in the resurrection. And for me, the whole biblical story of good and evil comes to rest here, in the resurrection. For the resurrection means that evil does not have the last word. God and his will of love have the last word. When evil has done its worst, in and through me as well as in and through others, there is always the possibility of a new beginning. "Behold, I make all things new." The promise to the people of Israel that they will be a blessing to the nations is not revoked or dead. It is empowered and enlivened by the resurrection of Christ from the dead.

So, "God so loved the world that he gave his only-begotten Son, that whosoever believes on him will not perish but obtain everlasting life" (John 3:16) means, in the framework of what we have been setting forth here, that the God who has disclosed his faithfulness and trustworthiness in the birth, life, death, and resurrection of Christ has freed you, at least in part, from your anxiety about who you are and what the future holds for you and thus has opened for you the possibility of trust and obedience and even of having something of the mind of Christ in you.

Biblical preaching therefore will rehearse this story week after week until it becomes a part of us, a part of our mind-set. It will not necessarily do in a single sermon what I have attempted to do here, to take a running start from the first chapters of Genesis and cruise on through to the Book of Revelation—although that might not be a bad idea once in a while, so that we can see the unfolding story as a whole for a change rather than just bits and pieces of it. But normally biblical preaching will deal with one incident in the story through the exploration of a text or passage. A lectionary which is developed in terms of the church year will help guarantee that all the major emphases in the biblical story will be dealt with over a year's preaching. (See chapter 5 above.)

This rehearsal of the biblical story will not be a rehearsal simply of what God did back there somewhere, for the battle between good and evil goes on, of course, and God's strategy for dealing with evil has not changed. Consequently, biblical preaching today will include judgment, or what is often called prophetic preaching. The purpose of this kind of prophetic preaching is to uncover evil and the potential for evil in even the best of us. (See chapter 6 above.)

But the major emphasis in biblical preaching, as in the biblical story, will be to evoke faith and trust in God's faithfulness and thus make possible obedience and salvation from the anxieties which cripple us. It will not talk *about* faith, because a relationship of trust and love is not created by talking about it. It will rather evoke it by calling attention to where God's faithfulness can be seen and experienced today and by pointing to his promises for the future.

But this is quite abstract. Sin wears many faces. What face is it wearing especially today? What is the *look* of evil in our world—and in us—today? Let's take a look at *our* stories in the light of the biblical story today.

Colin Williams, in a little study book on church renewal, wrote several years ago that *"the forms* of the renewed life in the church must be allowed to grow around all *the shapes of worldly need."*[4] This reflects the fact that the emphases in the biblical story shift in response to the human or worldly situation. The prophecy of Amos for example is directed to a people who were enjoying a long period of peace and prosperity but who were arrogant, corrupt, and highly diligent churchgoers and tithers. Consequently, the Word of the Lord on the lips of Amos to the people of Samaria is virtually an unrelenting word of judgment. There is little grace or promise or hope in the Book of Amos. On the other hand, the Word of the Lord on the lips of an unknown prophet of the Exile (Isaiah 40—55) is predominantly a word of comfort and hope addressed to the exiles in Babylon who, after fifty years, had just about despaired of God's love and care for them, of God's faithfulness. There is judgment too in this little prophecy, but the major emphasis is on God's love and grace as it is voiced in the opening lines of the prophecy "Comfort ye, comfort ye, my people; speak ye tenderly to Jerusalem" (Isa. 40:1-2). Differing human situations elicited different emphases in the Word of God addressed to them. Their stories were not unrelated to the way in which God addressed them.

The same thing holds true in postbiblical times. At the time of the Reformation the crying need of the people, symbolized in Luther's own experience, was how to find peace and acceptance in the face of an angry and wrathful God. So the central emphasis that Luther sought after and found in the biblical story was "justification by grace through faith." An angry God could not be placated by offerings or masses or self-flagellation or good works of any kind; God is a forgiving God, a reconciling God, whose grace overrules his wrath.

Well, what is the crying need among people today? I suspect that there are not a great many people lying awake nights tortured by the specter of an unforgiving and angry God. This is not to say that guilt is not a problem for a number of people. But I suspect that it is not the overriding problem for most of us. Indeed, one scholar observing the contemporary scene writes, "The New Testament's profound understanding of man's sin and suffering, and of judgment, are no longer comprehended. Man, with immortality in his soul, has certain inalienable rights. He has the right to a full life and a good life, and can legitimately claim them, and the necessity of God's judgment or of man's suffering is totally rejected, as a denial of that abundant life to which every human being is entitled."[5]

But I wonder if that is really an accurate reading of the contemporary situation. It may be true for some; it may be a superficial veneer for others. I suspect that underneath the surface most of us are not so self-assured or optimistic.

Perhaps the old cliché "an age of anxiety" is not a cliché after all. Perhaps it's closer to the truth. For piled on top of the common creaturely anxiety, the anxiety of recognized mortality, are all the massive and apparently unmanageable problems of our world: the population explosion and the shrinking food reserves leading to vast stretches of hunger and famine particularly in Asia and Africa; the energy crisis and the tension between the need for fuel and the ecological dangers of using certain kinds of energy. The unremitting tensions in southern Africa and the Middle East, the devastating worldwide inflation, and all the rest of it. So for a lot of us the problem is not so much an angry and wrathful God but the very real possibility that life is simply meaningless and hopeless, and that the problems we face are too overwhelming and unmanageable.

One understandable reaction to that situation is a flight to nostalgia. When the Book of the Month Club offers a record album of songs by Irving Berlin recorded by such nostalgic names as Ethel Merman, Billie Holiday, Fred Astaire, Kate Smith, and Mary Martin, I order it on the spot. My wife, watching the dreary news at six o'clock night after night, frequently comments, "I wish I had lived and died before 1913." So we turn the dial to "Upstairs, Downstairs" and go back to an older and (at some levels, at least) more gracious world.

Several contemporary theologians take a different approach to the problem. So Jürgen Moltmann:

> It is usually said that sin in its original form is man's wanting to be as God. But that is only one side of sin. The other side of such pride is hopelessness, resignation, inertia, and melancholy. From this arises the *tristesse* and frustration which fill all living things with the seeds of a sweet decay. Among the sinners whose future is eternal death in Rev. 21:8, the "fearful" are mentioned before unbelievers, idolaters, murderers, and the rest. Temptation then consists not so much in the titanic

desire to be as God but in weakness, timidity, weariness, not wanting to be what God requires of us.[6]

Moltmann further asserts that God honors us with his promises but that we do not believe ourselves capable of what is required of us. This is the sin, he says, which most profoundly threatens us as believers today. It is not the evil that we do but the good we leave undone; not my misdeeds but my omissions that accuse me; they accuse me, Moltmann says, of the lack of hope.[7]

Harvey Cox takes a less one-sided view but comes out at essentially the same place:

> In my view, the disaster which seems about to overtake us springs not from our brash cocksureness but from our cynical suspicion that there is nothing we can possibly do about it. I am not arguing that our sin is *solely* that of abdication, sloth, and cowardice rather than pride and swagger. I am saying that our sin is a curious *admixture* of both. It mingles arrogance and timidity, rushing in and sneaking away, *hubris* and *acedia*. I would further contend that in today's world, for most people, fear and impotence and self-pity seem more central.[8]

Furthermore, Cox finds the root of that situation in the ancient story of the fall in Genesis:

> If we read that old story carefully, we'll see it is not just a sin of pride. It is a sin of acedia. Eve shares with Adam the assignment of exercising mastery over all the creatures of the field. Her "original" misdeed was not eating the forbidden fruit at all. Before she reached for the fruit, she had already surrendered her position of power and responsibility over one of the animals, the serpent, and let it tell her what to do. Thus self-doubt, hesitant anxiety, and dependency actually preceded that fatal nibble which has fascinated us for so long and made us fuse sin with pride. Adam and Eve are the biblical Everyman and Everywoman. Their sin is our sin. It is not promethean. We do not defy the gods by courageously stealing the fire from the celestial hearth, thus bringing benefit to humanity. Nothing so heroic. We fritter away our destiny by letting some snake tell us what to do.[9]

Dr. Karl Menninger, not a professional theologian of course, comes to the same conclusion with respect to the shape of evil in life today: "The message is simple. It is that concern is the touchstone. Caring and relinquishing the sin of indifference. This recognizes acedia as the Great Sin, the heart of all sin."[10] Menninger talks of the overwhelming problems of our time and deals with them in terms of sin as "collective irresponsibility." He gives chapter and verse with respect to war, slavery, the ghettos, big corporations, handguns, population explosion, the American Indians, environment, affluence, and waste. These evils, he argues, are present because of the "Great Sin," acedia, lack of caring, anxiety, indifference, sloth.

Now if these witnesses are accurate in their diagnosis of evil in our time—and I think they are, both as I look around me and as I look into myself—then the emphasis in the Word addressed to the people of our time will be shaped around this worldly need. Biblical preaching will address itself to sin or evil as acedia.

And first of all it will expose the acedia within ourselves, the not caring, the refusal to accept responsibility, the temptation to give up and to give up hope. Actually, Menninger's book is just that, a fairly long sermon in the prophetic mood designed to expose the acedia in all of us. He wants to bring about recognition of sin and then calls us to repentance, to turn and accept our responsibility.

That may well be a necessary and salutary first step. But I need more hope than that, to accept the "responsibility" of which Menninger speaks. And preaching is far more than exhortation. Indeed, we have had far too much exhortation from pulpits down through the years. I have to know that it is *worth* accepting responsibility, that something good can come out of it, that it's more than just treading water or jogging in place, that there's a future to look forward to. I need to be told The Story, the story which tells me who I am, who God is, and what's to become of both of us.

And this is the purpose of the promises for the future which run all through the biblical story: the promise of a land, of the coming of a Messiah, of visions of jeweled cities, of eternal life, of the second coming of Christ. The purpose is not to entice us through an escape from the evils of this present world but rather, by giving us hope at the end of time, to enable us to engage in hopeful battles against evil in the present time. The biblical story, like any story, has a beginning, a middle (and that's where we are right now), and an end. But the end of the story is safely in God's hands. Life does win out over death in the end. God's good will for his world will defeat evil in the end. That's what all the gaudy promises and visions of the future in the biblical story are all about. All so that we can, as Paul urges us at the end of that magnificent chapter in 1 Corinthians 15, "be steadfast, immovable, always abounding in the work of the Lord, knowing that in the Lord your labor is not in vain" (1 Cor. 15:58).

I do not mean to suggest that such a hope is easy to come by, or that it readily issues in hopeful battles in the present. For hosts of people in our time, The Story is no longer believable or relevant. One of the major reasons for the evil of acedia in our time is precisely because we have lost or forgotten The Story. As Sam Keen puts it,

Until recent years, the keystone of personal identity was participation in the shared stories, legends, and myths of a tribe, nation, cult, or church. The past, present, and future of the individual were bound together by the memories and hopes of a people to which he belonged. With the birth of secular, pluralistic, technological society, a new type of person has emerged—the person without a story, the rootless, protean person living without the stability of a tradition which he remembers with pride or a future he awaits with longing. . . . There is little immediate possibility that a new overarching myth will emerge to provide a common structure for Western people in the way the Christian myth once did. Pluralism means that we no longer have common histories or shared hope.[11]

Sometimes I know that I feel as Sam Keen does here. But then I remember The Story—which is my story, our story—and The Story includes long, long periods of disillusionment and despair and hopelessness. The Psalms frequently give expression to it: "How long, O Lord, how long? Will you hide your face from me forever?" And part of the glory of The Story is that it records precisely those periods of disillusionment and despair and hopelessness as a witness to a people who hung in there and toughed it out when the going got rough because they would not give up their story of the faithfulness of God—even when everything around them seemed to deny it.

So biblical preaching today, along with all the other facets of the church's life of course, will keep bringing us back to The Story in the light of our stories and the story of our times. It will expose the acedia in us for the evil that it is; but even more it will prod our hope in the faithfulness of God to his promises as that faithfulness comes to light in the biblical story. We may not know how to worship very well any more or how to pray very well anymore or how to celebrate with abandon and integrity anymore; but if we can hang on to The Story, we shall not be lost.

There is a provocative story from Elie Wiesel:

When the great Rabbi Israel Baal Shem Tov saw misfortune threatening the Jews it was his custom to go into a certain part of the forest to meditate. There he would light a fire, say a special prayer, and the miracle would be accomplished and the misfortune averted. Later, when his disciple, the celebrated Magid of Mezritch, had occasion, for the same reason, to intercede with heaven, he would go to the same place in the forest and say, "Master of the Universe, Listen! I do not know how to light the fire, but I am still able to say the prayer." And again the miracle would be accomplished. Still later, Rabbi Moshe-Leib of Sasov, in order to save his people once more, would go into the forest and say, "I do not know how to light the fire, I do not know how to say the prayer, but I know the place and this must be sufficient." It was sufficient and the miracle was accomplished. Then it fell to Rabbi Israel of Rizhyn to overcome misfortune. Sitting in his armchair, his head in his hands, he spoke to God: "I am unable to light the fire and I do not know the prayer; cannot even find the place in the forest. All I can do is to tell the story, and this must be sufficient." And it was sufficient.[12]

NOTES

1. Amos Wilder, *The Language of the Gospel* (New York: Harper & Row, Publishers, 1964), p. 65.

2. B. Davie Napier, *Come Sweet Death* (Philadelphia: United Church Press, 1967), pp. 34-35. Used by permission.

3. Reinhold Niebuhr, *The Nature and Destiny of Man* (New York: Charles Scribner's Sons, 1943), 1:178ff.

4. Colin' Williams, *Where in the World* (New York: National Council of Churches, 1963), p. 59.

5. Elizabeth Achtemeier, *The Old Testament and the Proclamation of the Gospel* (Philadelphia: Westminster Press, 1973), p. 41.

6. Jürgen Moltmann, *Theology of Hope* (London: SCM Press, 1967), p. 22.

7. Ibid., p. 23.

8. Harvey Cox, *The Seduction of the Spirit* (New York: Simon & Schuster, 1973), p. 76.

9. Harvey Cox, *On Not Leaving It to the Snake* (New York: Macmillan Publishing Co., 1964), p. XIV.

10. Karl Menninger, *Whatever Became of Sin?* (New York: Hawthorn Books, 1973), p. 189.

11. Sam Keen, *To a Dancing God* (New York: Harper & Row, Publishers, 1970), p. 71.

12. Ibid., pp. 82-83, quoting from Elie Wiesel, *The Gates of the Forest* (New York: Holt, Rinehart & Winston, 1966).

8

The Irony and
Grammar of the Gospel

Morris J. Niedenthal

A layman asked a professor of preaching, "Why do I hear so much bad news from preachers? I thought they were supposed to preach good news." Since the professor did not know the layman personally, he immediately suspected that the layman wanted a neat and simple gospel which did not disturb him—or anyone else for that matter—a gospel that did not impinge directly on the tensions and crises of our common and public life, a gospel that nurtured a serene inner piety which evaded the grim and ugly realities of war, injustice, oppression, alienation, and poverty.

This was the professor's suspicion. But he was mistaken. The layman was deeply involved in trying to renew the church and trying to define the church's mission in the light of human needs. As a participant in a lay school of theology, he had probed the nature of the church and its missionary tasks. He was serving on a committee which discussed and devised strategies and structures for the church's mission through local congregations.

The professor was forced, therefore, to reconsider the layman's question, "Why do I hear so much bad news from preachers?" And his question enabled the professor to admit that he too had heard lots of bad news and that he had probably been guilty of spreading some of it himself.

Many people, lay and clerical alike, are tired of hearing that they have to be more involved in the affairs of the community, that they have to do their duties as parent, citizen, teacher, and church member. They are tired of hearing that they have to be more totally committed to Christ and to other people, whatever that means. They are tired of feeling a failure because they do not have an Atlas complex, which would enable them to shoulder the burdens of the world. People are tired of hearing all these admonitions. And some preachers are also tired of speaking them, not only because they are disturbing news but also because they clearly are bad news.

How is it possible, therefore, to speak good news without playing false to the rigorous character of the Scriptures? How is it possible to preach what H. H. Farmer called God's succor and his claim simultaneously?[1] These questions will be addressed and some constructive possibilities offered as we examine the irony and grammar of the gospel. Two modes of criticism, the ironic and the heroic, and two grammatical constructions of law and of gospel will be contrasted in terms of their suitability to the expression of God's claim.

Edwin M. Good, in his helpful study of *Irony in the Old Testament*, rightly points out that irony originates in the perception of an incongruity between what is and what ought to be.[2] It involves a conflict between pretense and reality. In classical Greek comedy this conflict was presented by two characters, one called the *aladzon,* the other the *eiron.* The *aladzon* was usually a pompous fool, a pretender who appeared to be greater, more heroic, than he actually was. A modern example of an *aladzon* is Donald Duck—thoroughly impressed with himself, usually humiliated and defeated, yet always ready to puff himself up again and renew his adventuresome living. The *eiron,* who is the *aladzon's* antagonist, is the sly, shrewd dissimulator who poses as less than he is. Recall some of Charlie Chaplin's troubles and escapades and you will have an image of the ironical man. The conflict between these two characters ends with the humiliation and defeat of the *aladzon* and the triumph of the *eiron.*

This type of irony, which exposes pretense and foolishness, is called comic irony. There is also of course tragic irony, but the concept of comic irony is especially illuminating. In the Bible God's man is often an ironical man, one who appears to be less than he is, and God's people are often presented as *aladzons,* pompous fools and pretenders. Moreover, the outcome of the conflict between the two often consists of the humiliation of the *aladzon* and the triumph of the *eiron.*

Amos, for example, appeared in Israel as an ironical man. He was only a shepherd, and he denied outright any claim of being a prophet or a prophet's son. Yet he spoke the Word of the Lord. He appeared as less than he was, and yet he spoke the words of judgment on Israel's proud pretensions.

Jesus is often presented as an ironical man. He appears to be less than he is. He is a carpenter from Nazareth, a wandering lay preacher, unordained, and yet he confounds the scribes and Pharisees and exposes their pretense and hypocrisy.

The Gospel of John contains motifs which are highly ironical. Observe for example the interesting interplay on the theme of the weak and the strong. Who gives the most direct witness to Christ? An outsider, a Samaritan woman. Who claims the body of Jesus after the crucifixion? The strong disciples? No, two weak ones—Nicodemus, who comes off quite badly earlier in the Gospel, and Joseph of Arimathea. Who is the indisputable victor in the Gospel? The man crucified. All are examples of an ironical treatment of a major motif in the Gospel of John.

Having noted a few examples of comic irony in the Bible, let us attempt to summarize its chief elements in four points:[3]

1. The perception of an incongruity between what is and what ought to be.
2. This perception is based on a vision or a revelation of truth.
3. Unlike the laughter which satisfies and pleases, ironic criticism hurts.
4. Ironic criticism aims to amend the incongruity, not to destroy or annihilate it (as in sarcasm).

Good concludes by noting two distinguishing characteristics of irony: "Irony is distinguished from other perceptions of incongruity by two characteristics. One is the means of statement, which we may describe as understatement or a method of suggestion rather than plain statement. The other is a stance in truth from which the perception comes."[4]

These characteristics differentiate irony from a heroic perception and statement. Whereas the ironic is usually expressed in understatement, the heroic tends toward overstatement. What is heroic overstatement in preaching? It can be the exaltation of hero figures. Or as applied to the listeners, people are implored to be courageous, to stand up and be counted, to get involved, to do their duties, to put their lives on the line, to become heroes of the faith. Note furthermore that the hero is made of his own self-determination and his own self-willing.

Now the biblical writers are certainly intent upon creating a faithful and courageous people, but their strategy often consists of using irony. They often shame people for their lack of faith, lack of courage, instead of describing hero figures for them to emulate. Consider Abraham, whom the Benedictus and St. Paul both identify as our father in the faith. He was not exactly a paradigm of courage and determination.

> Now there was a famine in the land. So Abraham went down to Egypt to sojourn there, for the famine was severe in the land. When he was about to enter Egypt, he said to Sarah his wife, "I know that you are a woman beautiful to behold; and when the Egyptians see you, they will say, "This is his wife"; then they will kill me, but they will let you live. Say you are my sister, that it may go well with me because of you, and that my life may be spared on your account. When Abraham entered Egypt the Egyptians saw that the woman was very beautiful. And when the princes of Pharaoh saw her, they praised her to Pharaoh. And the woman was taken into Pharaoh's house. And for her sake he dealt well with Abraham; and he had sheep, oxen, he-asses, menservants, maidservants, she-asses and camels.
>
> (Gen. 12:10–16)

Abraham our father; a hero, a brave man, a man of valor? Hardly! Fearing for his life and in order to save his skin, he instructed Sarah to tell the Egyptians a bald lie, one which had rather significant consequences. There is our "father," scared and dishonest, and every year as we read the lectionary of the church we need to remind ourselves and other Christian people that we are, as Paul said, Abraham's offspring. As if that reminder weren't enough, note further that one of the first lectures on ethics in Genesis is not given by our father in the faith but by that old pagan Pharaoh, who said to Abraham, "What is this you have done to me? Why did you not tell me that she was your wife? Why did you say, 'She is my sister,' so that I took her for my wife? Now then, here is your wife, take her and be gone" (Gen. 12:18–19). Abraham is no hero figure. He is a biblical figure, and his story is typical: the biblical writers often use irony instead of heroic overstatement.

If a hero is what we want, of course, we will probably prefer Socrates over Jesus, for Jesus is reported to have broken down and cried in the Garden of Gethsemane as he struggled with his impending death. The difference between them is that in his crying Jesus identified himself with us and we can identify ourselves with him.

The contrast between ironic and heroic statements is also evident in the parable of the good Samaritan. The irony of this parable is sharp and painful. A man asks what it is like to live under God's reign, to live in such a way that God has his way among people. And Jesus answers by telling the parable. The model which he holds up to the people of God is a pagan, a spiritual bastard, known to be outside the company of God's people. And in substance Jesus says, "Now look, an outsider can act humanly and decently. Shouldn't it be even more possible for you, my chosen people?" The understatement of Jesus in this parable is an essential aspect of the parable's meaning.

Moreover, this parable is a polemic against spectacular and heroic action, and this is all the more surprising because so many sermons on this parable make the Samaritan a hero figure. A crude caricature of many sermons on this text goes like this: "As Christians, we should love our neighbor. Since all people, and particularly those in need, are our neighbors, we should show no favoritism but love all people—our neighbor in southern Africa and the Middle East as well as our neighbor down the street." Now it would be quite spectacular and heroic for a person to love *all* people. But let's look at the text again. It doesn't say that the Samaritan loved *all* people. All it says is that the Samaritan had compassion on the needy man he bumped into, one he could do something for. Far from being a superhuman exhibit of Christian action, the Samaritan's action was simple and ordinary. I think the parable of the good Samaritan describes a simple, unspectacular *human* act and calls it godly action and service. And that is precisely why the priest and Levite come off so badly; not because they lacked heroic courage, for after all, they might have said, we are just ordinary blokes, a bit cowardly at heart. They come off badly because they lacked any simple human concern and compassion.

What is true of this parable is generally true of the Samaritan tradition in the Gospels. It is helpful to trace the references to the Samaritans in the Gospels in order to see how Samaritans are held up as models for the people of God. And I suspect that as we translate the meaning of these passages today, we should see ourselves and the church identified in the scribes and Pharisees, and the Samaritans identified in unchurched people around us.

The difference between ironic statements and heroic statements reflects different stances in truth. Ironic perception and statement acknowledge and affirm the novelty and surprise of God's grace. Irony calls attention to and celebrates that amazing grace of God which exposes religious pretension and which utilizes sinners in the advancement and fulfillment of his purpose. Ironic perception and statement are appropriate to a stance which affirms that God loves and justifies sinners. Furthermore, ironic criticism cuts so deeply not because it shows up our failure to achieve heroic stature but because it goes straight to our denial of ourselves as human beings. Irony therefore affirms human beings in the concrete actuality of each: a mixture of weakness and strength, cowardice and courage, sin and faith.

Heroic perception and statement on the other hand tend to become legalistic, because they glorify human courage, human self-willing determination, and human achievement. Heroic criticism cuts at the point of our failure to become what we should be ideally, not our failure to become what we are. It criticizes people by saying that they should be *more* courageous, *more* involved, *more* committed. Heroism therefore affirms only human strength and cannot accommodate human weakness.

The preacher needs to learn the distinction between the ironic and the heroic modes of perception and their statements. The ironic is open to the novelty of grace and its operation; the heroic on the other hand often becomes legalistic. Both perceptions are critical, but they differ in the manner and the point of criticism. (Even the title of the sermon at the end of this chapter, "Disturbed by Joy," is ironic. But notice the other ironies in this sermon.)

The means and manner of statement which were briefly discussed in relation to understatement and overstatement can be further clarified by examining the grammar of the gospel. The theological categories of law and gospel are commonly used in theological construction, the law being understood as that which expresses the unconditional will of God which convicts people of their sin and opens them to receive the gospel of God's mercy, forgiveness, and freedom. The law, it is sometimes said, drives people to Christ. The gospel, then, is God's gracious gift of mercy and compassion. Whereas the language of the law speaks of demand, necessity, proof, and achievement, the language of the gospel speaks of gift, freedom, acceptance, reconciliation, and hope.

This neat distinction between demand and gift needs to be reappraised. It can imply that only the law makes a claim or a demand. If this were true, it would mean that any preacher who lays a claim on a congregation must be preaching the law. The truth however may rather be that both the law and the gospel make claims but that they do so in different ways. Herein lies the difference between the grammar of the law and the grammar of the gospel.[5]

The grammar of the law is most apparent in the conditional sentence: If this, then that. For example: If you repent, then you will be forgiven. If you become more deeply involved, then you will be more truly Christian. If you love your neighbor, then you will be a Christian. If you have faith, then you will know God's presence. If you honor your father and mother, then you will have long life on the earth. If you're a good little boy, then I'll take you to the movies. If this, then that.

Notice the effects and implications of the grammar of the law:

1. The future is made to depend entirely upon the past. The future in the will clause, "then you will be forgiven," is totally dependent upon the accomplishment of the if clause, the condition, namely, "if you repent." Moreover, from the standpoint of the future will clause, the conditional clause is past tense. The damnable thing about the law is that it always rivets people to their past, either to their sins or to their accomplishments and merits. And since our past is always a mixed bag of successes and failures, our future is filled with anxiety and fear. When our future is made to depend entirely upon our past, then our future is death. For the past is fixed, dead; it cannot be changed. Therefore no new beginning is ever possible. The end of the law is despair and death. That the Apostle Paul saw this clearly is particularly evident in his treatment of the law in the Epistle to the Romans.

2. The grammar of the law is safe and simplistic. If the future promise does not materialize, it is of course because the condition was not properly met. A student comes into my office and confides in me that he is greatly disturbed and upset because he no longer senses

God's presence in his life. He prays, but he is not at all certain that there is anyone listening to his prayers. I respond by affirming his feelings and experience and by pointing out that many people, even some notable saints, go through very similar experiences. Then I suggest to him that the root of his problem is his inability to believe strongly enough that God is really present with him. The student looks at me incredulously. For he already *knows* that *if* he believed strongly enough, then he would sense God's presence. But that is no help to him; what I have said is no more than a restatement of his problem, which is simply that he cannot believe.

3. This leads to a third implication of the grammar of the law. It presupposes strength but does nothing to create it. "If you have faith" presupposes faith but does nothing to create it. "If you become involved" presupposes the strength to become involved but does nothing to create that strength. "If you love your neighbor" presupposes the ability and freedom to love but creates neither the ability nor the freedom to love.

So much then for the grammar of the law as expressed in the conditional sentence. It might be revealing and helpful for us as preachers to check the number of conditional sentences in our sermons; this would be one way to determine how much law is actually being preached. Furthermore, sometimes an entire sermon and not only an individual sentence will have a grammatical effect: If A, then B. And that is the grammar of the law.

The grammar of the gospel on the other hand stresses the declarative clause and sentence: Because A, therefore B. It is important to recognize that the clause which is introduced with *therefore* contains an imperative. It makes a claim.

The twelfth chapter of Romans begins, "I appeal to you, therefore, brethren, by the mercies of God, to present your bodies as a living sacrifice, holy and acceptable to God, which is your spiritual worship." The first eleven chapters of Paul's Letter are a *because*. *Because* God has decisively delivered people from the curse of sin, the bondage of the law, and the body of death in Jesus Christ, *therefore* present your bodies as living sacrifices. The apostle makes a claim: present your bodies.

Or consider Jesus' words to the paralytic: "Son, your sins are forgiven. Get up and walk." *Because* your sins are forgiven, *therefore* get up and walk.

The first commandment, obviously a law, is important for us in the present discussion because of its grammatical form. "I am the Lord your God, who brought you out of the land of Egypt, out of the house of bondage. You shall have no other gods before me." Grammatically this reads, "*Because* I am the Lord your God, who brought you out of the land of Egypt, out of the house of bondage, *therefore* you shall have no other gods before me."

Consider now some of the effects and implications of the grammar of the gospel:

1. The grammar of the gospel opens a new and different future by declaring an action of God which alters the meaning of the past. Put another way, the grammar of the gospel opens the future to a new possibility by overcoming the limitations of the past. The paralytic was faced with a new possibility by virtue of the fact that the limitations of his past were overcome.

2. The grammar of the gospel does not presuppose strength but seeks to create it by ministering to need and weakness. It would have been foolish and cruel to have said to the paralytic, "If you have faith, then you will be able to get up and walk." The paralytic's needs had to be attended to before he had a ghost of a chance of getting up off his pallet and walking.

Perhaps an analogy will make the point clearer. Children raised in homes where love is genuine and where their needs and weaknesses are accepted and attended to are very different from children who feel that they must prove themselves worth loving, they must conceal their weaknesses and failures or face rejection. The former relationship seeks to create strength, the latter presupposes it.

How, then, can we preach that genuinely good news which is nevertheless faithful to Scripture? How can we preach God's succor and his claim simultaneously? We contend that the ironic mode of perception and statement will allow for both the affirmation of God's novel graciousness and also the criticism of human pretense and foolishness which prevents people from being truly human. Moreover, the grammatical construction and effect of law are quite distinct from those of gospel, and only the grammar of the gospel truly expresses both God's succor and his claim. The irony and grammar of the gospel may thus encourage and enable preachers to celebrate that foolishness of God which is wiser than the constructions of human minds.

NOTES

1. H. H. Farmer, *The Servant of the Word* (Philadelphia: Fortress Press, 1964), p. 46.

2. Edwin M. Good, *Irony in the Old Testament* (Philadelphia: Westminster Press, 1965).

3. Ibid., pp. 25–33.

4. Ibid., pp. 30–31.

5. Cf. Robert W. Jenson, *Story and Promise* (Philadelphia: Fortress Press, 1973), pp. 6-9.

9

Moving from
The Story to Our Story

Ronald J. Allen and
Thomas J. Herin

It is Monday morning. The glow of yesterday's service and sermon has faded. Alone in the study, I contemplate next week's sermon.

What portion of the total biblical story—what text—will speak most appropriately to those of us in this church this week? I have learned that no set rule can automatically answer that important question. We have been following the lectionary, but we have discovered that the Word of the Lord does not always come in the prescribed readings. The pericope this week is 1 Cor. 8:1-13, an odd tract about eating meat which has been offered to idols. That is one possibility for a text.

But today other options come to mind—options deriving from the lives of the preacher and of the listeners. Recently I saw a movie that triggered more than a little reflection, and I have wanted to explore some of its impact with the congregation. That desire is not easily suppressed. The third and fourth grade church-school class has been growing seeds in hard-packed soil, in rocky soil, in soil covered with weeds, and in loamy, fertile soil. The experience of the class in watching the seeds grow (and try to grow) has made the parable of the sower and the soils (Mark 4:2-8) come alive, and I have wanted to share some of that excitement with the whole church. It would be important for all of us to do so. A rumor is afoot that one of the local factories may close and leave several members of the church out of work; also several Chicano families have moved into the city of late, and I have heard some grumbling—and sensed some fear—around town. Those are important things. If I ignore them and preach about meat offered to idols, what purpose would I be serving?

And suppose I do preach—as I usually do—from a single text? What do I do when no one passage seems to address a particular local need sufficiently? This is what happened when our first child was to be baptized and I decided to preach on the meaning of baptism. As I reflected on the significance of this event for my wife and me and as I studied the Bible and the Christian tradition on the subject, I realized that the practice is rooted in the whole fabric of the gospel more deeply and clearly than in any single text. So I organized my sermon topically and interwove numerous biblical passages with my experience of the moment. Edmund Steimle does much the same thing in "Disturbed by Joy" (see the sermon below) when he draws on the testimony of all the resurrection accounts to illumine an experience both ancient and modern.

After considerable rumination about which idea holds the liveliest possibilities for next week's sermon, I realize that I need more time to reflect further on the implications of the movie. As for the seeds, they are just starting to sprout: maybe it would be good to wait until the plants mature fully, as they do in the parable. With a little more time, perhaps some of the kids could be interviewed for the sermon. The plant closing is still a rumor. And finally, although Eph. 2:11–19 with its emphasis on Christ's breaking down the dividing wall of hostility between Jews and Gentiles has come to mind as an appropriate biblical address to the community's attitude toward the Chicanos, the congregation has actually been rather accepting of our new neighbors. None of these ideas seems quite ready. Perhaps they can be put on the back burner to simmer a bit longer.

So I read through 1 Corinthians 8 again, and now several intriguing features catch my attention. What kind of "knowledge" do the Corinthian Christians have? What is all this business about idols and "many gods and lords"? How does one Christian's eating meat become a stumbling block to another Christian?

At times my own fascination with a text has seemed sufficient reason to choose it for a forthcoming sermon. Other texts at other times have come to have special meaning for both me and my hearers, each pressing its own special claim. There are no surefire methods which will insure that a given text will come to life. But I have found that whenever I am really experiencing a part of the biblical story as *my* story, the chances are greater that my hearers will experience it as theirs. My sermon may contain many personal references or none at all, but my hearers will know how much my own story is affected.

At present the phrase "many gods and lords" intrigues me. Just last night at the hamburger stand on the edge of town some young people from our youth group came running up to my car with a tract which had been handed to them on the parking lot. In bold, black print it announced that the world is rife with demons and that the reader of the tract had better watch out lest she or he become a habitation for demons. The young people were laughing about the tract and making fun of the idea of demons. I recollect further that occasionally someone comments about his or her daily horoscope, and also that this morning's mail brought notice of a parapsychology meeting at a local college. Recently some reporters in England have even been trying to televise a ghost. There does seem to be interest in the air about extrahuman forces in the world. This may be a time, then, to marry 1 Corinthians 8 with this particular congregation.

Once the text is chosen, where do we go? For me, no single method consistently sets the process off on a fruitful start. On more than one occasion a morning—or two or even three—has passed with the bird's nest outside the study window attracting more attention than the sermon.

Even then, however, when a vacant stare was the most that I could manage consciously, I have been surprised at what had apparently been fermenting unconsciously, and came to the surface when I began to outline or write. Thus I try to get the process of preparation under way early in order to allow plenty of time for text, images, and ideas to percolate.

When dealing with a text which is narrative in form, for example the encounter of the prophet Nathan with King David (2 Sam. 12:1-14), I will customarily read the vignette several times, each time identifying myself with a different character. When the text is more obviously didactic, for example the Sermon on the Mount, I try to seat myself among those to whom Jesus was speaking. When reading passages that obviously bespeak physical action, I act out the action so that I can feel it in my whole person. (One morning my secretary was startled by an explosive clap of the hands followed by a shout as I read Ps. 47:1!)

Today however I begin by reading the text aloud several times, each time giving emphasis to different words and ideas. Reading aloud causes the mind to slow down, to focus on particular phrases and words, and sometimes to pick up meanings which the eye skips, especially if the passage is a familiar one.

After making a few notes, I take down the Greek New Testament and the Greek-English lexicon and translate. I do not turn to the original language in order to be able to sprinkle the sermon with such impressive remarks as "Now in the Greek, it *really* says . . ." Rather, I have found that like reading aloud, reading the text in the original language is more likely to allow me to feel its power, to sense its inner structure, and to pick up the force of particular images and phrases.

A flag goes up for instance when in translating verse 1 I find in the lexicon that the word which is rendered "build up" is nearly always used by Paul to refer to the building up of the community. Thus "knowledge" destroys community but love builds it up.

One of my ministerial colleagues did not take Hebrew but did study Spanish. So when the sermon grows from an Old Testament text, she reads it in Spanish as well as in several different English translations. Often the Spanish version helps bring the text alive in new and surprising ways, and highlights the movement and structure of the passage.

After reading and translating and before consulting any commentaries, I make notes of my own impressions of the text, the problems it poses, the things it seems to say to my situation, and any examples or images that pop into mind. Today the notes take the form of questions: "What was the situation in Corinth which caused Paul to take quill in hand? What is the 'knowledge' which gets Paul so worked up? Who are the many 'gods and lords' of verse 5? Why should my actions be restricted because of someone else's 'hang-ups' (v. 13)?"

Week by week the initial questions are always different and are sparked by the text itself. Revelation 8 left me asking, "Are there *really* going to be angels blowing trumpets and causing great hunks of the universe to come unglued?" John 10 was at first offensive: "Does the Jesus of John describe *me* as a sheep—a stupid, smelly animal which mindlessly follows other sheep around and which can see only five feet in front of its face?'' In reading Amos 5 I felt as though my eyes had struck a theological pothole when they bumped into the phrase

> Seek me and live,
>   but do not seek Bethel.

"Does Amos mean that sometimes God is not found in Bethel, the 'First Christian Church' of ancient Israel? Can he mean that if we are to find God, we sometimes need to get away from religious people and the church?''

After letting the questions simmer for a day, I turn to the commentaries and other exegetical tools. The aim in doing this is not so much to gather material for the sermon as it is to get a communal check on my reading of the text. Is my interpretation fair to the text in its full literary and historical context? Is it in line with what other trained and sensitive readers have discovered? By this time I may find that the sermon is taking a quite different direction than I first thought it would.

By experience I have learned that no single series of commentaries (such as The Interpreter's Bible, Hermeneia, The Anchor Bible, The Old Testament Library, Harper's New Testament Commentaries, Proclamation Commentaries) contains uniformly high-quality exegesis for each book of the Bible; the individual contributions vary greatly in quality. Therefore, like some pastors, I have selectively accumulated individual volumes from different series. In addition to the commentaries, I may use such aids as *Theological Dictionary of the New Testament* and Proclamation: Aids for Interpreting the Lessons of the Church Year, works on the background of the biblical world, theologies of the Bible, and a concordance.

Exegesis is not an exact surgical procedure practiced on an inert text; the text is not like an anesthetized body on which a surgeon operates. My text is rather more like a visitor from outside my immediate but often quite limited world of experience. And whether he is an old friend or a virtual stranger, I have opened the door to him at this time, and I now want to hear his news, whether it calms me or upsets me. I also want to ask him some tough questions, to acknowledge my own hopes and fears in his presence, and to get to know him well enough to introduce him to my Christian companions. Rather than manipulating or using or talking *about* my guest in public, I want to enable my comrades to hear him on his own terms.

Most biblical texts are themselves stories, or like the laws of Deuteronomy, they have been set within a narrative framework in their present canonical form. In order for me to enter fully into the story of the text it is often helpful to read the text as story. In the case of the parable of the father and two sons (Luke 15:11-32) I might ask, "How would we usually expect a situation like the one between the father and the sons to develop? What turns of events are surprising? How does the narrator draw us into the story? Why do we identify with certain characters?"

We can ask similar questions even of didactic and epistolary forms. For example, "How do I expect that Paul will address the Corinthians? How does his response confirm or surprise me? What is the internal movement of the passage—how does Paul get from one point to another?"

When interpreting a pericope, I have found that the most real and lively sermons have come when I identify myself with the persons to whom the text is addressed. On first reading the text, as I have already mentioned, I try to read it from the perspective of the different persons involved in order to see how the text feels from the position of each character. But when I form the sermon itself, I identify myself and my hearers with those who needed to hear the word from the biblical writer. Thus I identify myself, and us, not with God but with the people to whom God speaks; I see myself not as Jesus but as one among those whom Jesus heals or to whom he speaks; I am not Jeremiah, flailing away at the congregation; I am among the people to whom Jeremiah's prophecy is directed.

A key question is, How am I like them? What in our world functions in the same way that the "gods and lords" functioned in the world of Paul and the Corinthians? How am I like the woman at the well? How am I like Job's friends? How is our church like the Israel to whom the Book of Hosea was addressed?

In turning to the text of the week now, I find the commentaries suggesting that the Corinthian church was divided into two camps over the question of eating meat which had been offered to an idol. Who were these two groups? One was characterized by "possession of knowledge" (8:1). "Knowledge" in Corinth referred not to a command of factual information but to a "spiritual secret" or "religious insight." Those who "possess knowledge" eat meat which has been offered to idols. Others in the church however are offended by that practice.

Why should it be offensive to the second group to see the first eat such meat? Is it so different from gulping down a hamburger with all the trimmings? Ah! To the pagan Corinthians the idols were not just statues of clay or metal; they represented gods or lords who exercised power and authority in the world. The second group believed that eating meat which had been sacrificed before an idol placed one in the sphere of that idol's power. By contrast, the first group displayed bumper stickers reading, "All of Us Possess Knowledge" (8:1); they believed that "an idol has no real authority" (RSV "existence"). Therefore they felt no qualms about eating the same meat by which their comrades felt themselves defiled.

How does Paul respond, and to whom? Paul agrees with the first group that eating idol-meat does not affect one's relationship to God. However, Paul perceives that there *are* influences in the world other than God (8:5). Paul suggests that those who feel entirely free to eat meat offered to idols should nevertheless exercise care in the use of their liberty. For if they act in such a way that their liberty becomes a stumbling block to those who are unliberated, the unliberated person is destroyed (!) and the first person sins in causing that downfall.

In concluding, Paul does not give a command but places himself in the pew of the first group: "Therefore, if food is the cause of my brother's or sister's falling, I will never eat meat lest I cause my brother or sister to fall" (8:13). Paul's approach suggests a mode of sharing the story. For Paul does not reach the climax of the argument and wag his finger. Instead, he turns to the story of his own life and what he would do if he were in their situation.

The exegesis has revealed several surprises. From 8:9 we can infer that Paul is counseling prudent use of one's freedom: it is all right to eat meat which is offered to idols so long as the wrong persons don't see it or hear about it. Isn't that a backhanded way of describing hypocrisy?

Paul's conclusion (8:13) is likewise perplexing. Where do we draw the line in restraining our behavior for the benefit of our sisters and brothers? Many preachers have no compunction about drinking or smoking, and they read the Bible through the lens of the historical-critical method. But if we live in a conservative area, how far can we go in manifesting elements of a life-style that is offensive to the genuine piety of some Christians? On the other hand, however, if for fear of causing offense to someone (and therefore causing a crack in the church) I take no action at all, what good purpose can *that* serve?

In the course of the exegesis, then, at least three sermon possibilities have bubbled to the surface: (1) the interplay of "gods" and God in our world; (2) the question of whether it is permissible (even laudable) to be one way with one group and another way with another group for the benefit of the church; (3) the problem of restraining my freedom out of respect for the conscience of another.

The problem of multiple sermons arising from one text is not uncommon. Note for example Deuteronomy 34, a description of the death of Moses on which Joseph Sittler's "The View from Mount Nebo" is based (see the sermon above). Despite the abundance of themes generated by the pericope, Sittler has taken one idea and honed it. He obviously does not try to say all that he knows about the passage.

As I mull over the three possibilities, the first choice begins to emerge as the most promising. I feel, partly intuitively, that the time is right in our local situation: there are indications of interest, however vaguely articulated, in the possible influence of "outside" forces on our lives (the tract, the horoscopes, the parapsychology meeting, the ghost).

The other sermon ideas may well speak powerfully on other occasions, so I copy them into a sermon notebook, along with whatever images, examples, and questions they have stimulated. And I shall thumb through that notebook from time to time and keep those ideas warm until the right moment comes to bring them to a boil.

For the present, however, I try to express the thrust of the present sermon in one sentence: "Like the Corinthians, we experience the influence and authority of unseen 'powers' in the world, but we can be freed from them as we live under the lordship of Jesus." All other material to which I attend as the sermon comes together will be judged by whether or not it will directly help this sentence grow into a lively, sensitive, thoughtful whole. Material which will not be illuminating this week is either copied into the notebook or discarded.

I live with the sermon idea and carry it—not always consciously—wherever I go. Connections between the life of the text and the life of the church often appear in unexpected places: reading a magazine in the barbershop, shredding lettuce for supper, driving on the freeway, visiting in the hospital.

Although my bookshelf contains volumes of "homiletical aids" donated by well-meaning friends, I seldom use them. Usually they sound canned, stale, and truncated when abstracted from the context which gave them birth. I do find stimulation in the published preaching of some other preachers because their images and illustrations and creative approaches to a given text will often trigger my own creative powers.

On Wednesday morning I try to organize the material clearly. How can The Story and our story (and stories) be woven together so that new light is shed on both?

Some texts themselves suggest an outline and an organizational pattern. This is especially true of narrative texts, such as sagas, miracle stories, controversy stories, parables. The sermon can simply unfold in the same scenes and development as the drama.

Other texts, although not narrative in form, nonetheless can help organize material if we simply take the structure of the text as an outline, for example the diatribe form common in Paul's letters. Other forms, such as law codes, prophetic oracles, and wisdom sayings, presuppose for their understanding certain stories or situations in the ancient communities of the faithful. It is sometimes vivid and useful to sketch the story out of which the saying grew rather than to plunk it down in the pulpit like a chicken without feathers. In its full context we see and feel its power as part of a real human story, and not simply as a disembodied spiritual or ethical principle. On other occasions I use as an outline the actual process of sermon preparation, from first reaction through exegesis. The sermon is thus molded explicitly by the contours of human experience.

This week an image from my personal experience gives the sermon its form, much as Edmund Steimle's memory of hurricane Hazel became his means of structuring and presenting a sermon on Luke 2:1-20 (see "The Eye of the Storm" above). I was walking through a shopping mall, noticing the sights, sounds, smells, and scenes (some humorous, some boring, others pathetic), when I found myself— only thirty minutes after supper, my belly still bloated—purchasing a large box of popcorn. The words came to me suddenly, "Why am I doing this?"

Stepping back, I saw that the popcorn popper was equipped with a fan to direct the aroma of fresh-popped corn into the hall. Above the machine was a sign which I had not consciously noticed which read, "SAVE . . . on a giant box of fresh popcorn." As I looked down the hallway, another sign appeared which had not attracted attention as we were walking along, which said, "You've almost made it . . ." and which pictured a handful of fresh, buttered popcorn. With the photographer's retouching, the picture looked more appetizing than the real thing. Of course! I was encountering one of those unnoticed and unconsidered "lords."

As I walked along I turned the incident over in my mind. "If anyone were to ask me, I would insist that I am not about to fall victim to the ploys of advertising. I buy strictly on the merits of the merchandise. Oh, occasionally I may splurge a little, but that is when I really want to have a good time. Tonight, however, my purchase of popcorn was not really a matter of conscious choice." As the walk proceeded, other signs now attracted attention: "Coke . . . the *real* thing." "The answer is Audi." "Gee," I thought, "if the answer is Audi, we're in trouble!"

Later, in counseling, the words of a parishioner debilitated by a problem with alcohol flashed true: "I just don't have any power over my urge to drink, and when I am drinking, I become a different person." I began to think of other ways in which our thoughts and actions are influenced by powers outside ourselves, powers which appear to be "invisible."

The experience with the popcorn becomes the major image to hold the sermon together, and elements of the Corinthian story are interwoven. An outline takes shape.

With an outline in hand I turn to writing the manuscript. I nearly always prepare a full manuscript. Some time ago I switched from an outline to a manuscript. For in those earlier days the sermons tended to go on much past the twenty-minute attention span of most adults, and on one notorious occasion I kept trying to stretch out the points because I was afraid the sermon would be too short. In the end, it was padded to thirty-five sleepy minutes. The manuscript encourages me to construct the sermon more tightly and to use language and images more carefully and precisely, especially when a particular image seems to open up a text as the warm sun opens a blossom.

I can use a manuscript as many preachers use notes. A neighboring pastor found that if she uses a manuscript she reads it, often in a monotone; so she has switched to an outline. Another minister in our city writes a manuscript, then outlines it, and then throws away both manuscript and outline. And still another preacher has the discipline to prepare a sermon entirely in his head, using almost no written notes. Each of these last two likes to roam about the chancel while preaching, unencumbered by either the notes or the pulpit.

I have also noticed that my style in the pulpit changes as I change and as the situation of preaching changes. A conversational style of preaching, warm and real in a church-in-the-round, cannot always be transferred to a Gothic church which echoes. My whole style of preaching is not up for grabs every week, but I am open to fresh and promising changes.

One element of preaching which cannot be orchestrated is the chemistry of the moment of actual delivery. Sermons which on Friday read like exploding dynamite have fizzled on Sunday, and a message which seemed as exciting as taking out the trash has sparkled. And it is extremely difficult to predict how any one will be received.

I have learned that in the whole process of sermon preparation— from choosing a text or topic, to hearing what that particular text says to my particular pastoral situation, to finding a form that fits content and preacher and congregation—I am ultimately preparing a person rather than a product. As preachers we are getting ready to share "not only the gospel of God but also our own selves" (1 Thess. 2:8). So my body temperature, my blood pressure, and what I ate for breakfast may well color the conversation that my people and I have with the Scriptures.

Yet when my hearers sense that a part of the biblical story has indeed become *my* story, they are invited to make connections with their own stories. They are not compelled to enter into what is happening for me, and there can be no guarantee that they will. But seeing and hearing, in their preacher, a living person who is in touch with real feelings and who is actually experiencing connections between God's ongoing Story and his own gives them example and encouragement and hope.

10

The Fabric of the Sermon

Edmund A. Steimle

The sermon, of course, is one form of proclamation. And the nature of Christian proclamation is determined by the nature of revelation, the nature of the revelatory and consequently redemptive activity of God as witnessed to in the Bible. The Bible, therefore, is the source for the content of proclamation. But proclamation is not merely a recital of God's mighty acts in the past. In proclamation (preaching) God is actually present here and now making his claim and offering his grace.

This revelatory and redemptive activity of God combines both action and the interpretation of the action, both deed and word. God reveals himself through his mighty deeds recorded in the Bible, to be sure. But the deeds, the action, would be meaningless apart from the interpretation of the action in the words of prophets, apostles, Christ himself, and indeed of the church down to the present time. Thus the climactic event in God's revelation of himself—the life, death, resurrection of Christ and the coming of the Spirit—centers in an action. But without interpretation, the action would remain an enigma. Consequently if proclamation (preaching) is to reflect in its content its biblical source, it will combine action and the interpretation of the action.

It is relatively easy to see how proclamation can reflect the interpretation of God's action in the world, for proclamation is talking about God and his ways with his people. But how can a multiplication of words in the pulpit actually become a deed? In what sense can action take place in the preaching event, and especially in a world surfeited with words?

Perhaps a closer examination of the Bible, not only with respect to its essential content but also with respect to the form in which that content is conveyed, may give us a clue. Amos Wilder, in his provocative little book *The Language of the Gospel* (to which I would acknowledge my debt for the basic approach in this chapter) notes that to draw a distinction between what the early Christians said and how they said it is to draw a false distinction. He writes:

> Form and content cannot long be held apart. . . . The character of the early Christian speech forms should have much to say with regard to our understanding of Christianity and its communication today. We may well go back to the fountainhead of the gospel in this respect also. This is not to be taken in a trite sense; for example, that because Jesus used parables we also should use illustrations from life, or because the New Testament has a place for poetry we also should use it. All this is true. The question is rather, what kind of story? What kind of poetry? Nor should we feel ourselves enslaved to biblical models whether in statement, image, or form. But we can learn much from our observations as to the appropriate strategies and vehicles of Christian speech and then adapt them to our own situation. It is significant, for example, how large a part the dramatic mode has in the faith of the Bible and in its forms of expression, even though we find no theatre-art as we know it in the Bible or among early believers. The important role of religious drama in our churches today has, nonetheless, very specific justification in biblical theology and in the New Testament rhetorical forms.[1]

Thus if the content of Christian proclamation down through the years and today is biblical through and through, the form of Christian proclamation should also be biblical through and through. As Wilder suggests, "Any human language represents a special kind of order imposed upon existence." The biblical character of preaching therefore will determine not only its content but its form or, to use the term used as the title for this chapter, its fabric, which is to say, its structure, language, grammar, and imagery. (See for example chapter 8 above.) No doubt the general principles of rhetoric and public address may be helpful in mastering the art of oral communication, but they are subservient to the basic kind of rhetoric used in the Bible because the biblical rhetoric is wedded in form to its content. The fabric or texture of the sermon, as well as its content, will be determined by its biblical roots. For one thing, little or no surprise is evident in much preaching today. And yet the Word of God as witnessed to in the Bible brought surprise, consternation, anger, and rejection, as well as the joy of an angel chorus flooding the sky with song. Today, as one college student put it to me bluntly concerning the sermons he had heard, "If you've heard one, you've heard 'em all." This same bored reaction is reported by other observers. Martin Marty for example writes: "The faith can be dismissed without a hearing because Americans feel that they already know what it has to say. A culture like our own, shaped as it is in no small part by Protestantism, so identifies itself with that faith as culture but not as revelation that it expects no surprises."[2]

To counteract this deep and widespread ennui with respect to preaching, let us consider some of the characteristics of the form of the biblical witness which, if understood and given their head on Sunday mornings, might bring preaching alive.

First, the fabric of the biblical witness is completely and thoroughly secular, even perhaps when it sounds just the opposite in our twentieth-century ears. One of the more intriguing sermons I've read in recent years, one blessed with the element of surprise, was prepared for the Sunday in the church year commemorating St. Michael and All Angels. This would hardly offer an appropriate theme for the task of "the servant church in the world," one might think, and would be peculiarly inappropriate for an academic community to which the sermon was originally addressed. And yet after dealing in depth and with considerable wit with the problems of angels in the biblical record, the sermon cited Jesus' use of contemporary angelology as an unmistakable mark of the secular man that he was, a man totally immersed in the images and thought patterns of his age. And then the sermon went on from there.

I suppose that our familiarity with the fabric of the Bible has dulled our sensitivity to its sheer secularity. In the Old Testament the story of God's dealings with his people is studded with battles and sex and death and shady deals, with the plight of poverty-stricken widows and the suffering of the innocent, with markets and temples and idols and courts and deserts and cities. And this is where the "spiritual" is discerned, not apart from it. The story is told as if God were at work in the world, which of course and indeed he was.

The fabric of the New Testament is not essentially different, despite our misguided efforts to spiritualize it. Jesus comes into the world and stays there until he dies, and the gospels are records of God in Christ at work in the world. When Jesus uses the parables as a teaching device, he uses essentially secular, worldly stories. They were not heard as "Bible stories" as we have come to think of them. As Wilder points out, "Jesus, without saying so, by his way of presenting man in the parables, shows that for him man's destiny is at stake in his ordinary creaturely existence, domestic, economic, and social. This is the way God made him. The world is real. Time is real. Man is a toiler and an 'acter' and a chooser. The parables give us this kind of humanness and actuality."[3]

When you come to Paul and his reflections on the meaning of all this, the fabric is of a different order and consequently has provided vast problems for preachers ever since. But even Paul with his theological reflections uses thoroughly secular images for the central mysteries of the gospel. The image of redemption for example comes directly out of the slave market. Gerhard Ebeling sums it all up by saying, "All talk of God is worldly talk of God."[4]

Now if this be so, then the fabric of the sermon will be worldly, secular, through and through. "The language of Canaan," the blasphemous smoke screen which hides and distorts the gospel because it implies that the reality of it all can be known only in terms of the first century, will be replaced by the actual language of the Bible, the *true* "language of Canaan," the language and idioms of the people where they are, the vernacular, the vocabulary of the world in which we live.

This means in explicit terms that the sermon will be studded with allusions to the facts and fancies and news events which make the newspapers: international tensions and conglomerates, Northern Ireland, the Middle East, the energy crisis, abortion, the obituary columns, stock-market fluctuations, inflation, legislative tangles in Congress, Dear Abby, black power and white power-structures, the daily horoscope, Peanuts, the NFL or the NBA . . . as well as with allusions to the facts and fancies and happenings which rarely if ever make the newspapers: the meaningless, sordid, and lonely waiting for death in a sleazy nursing home, the bleak despair when by some trick of the economy a fifty-five-year-old man is laid off, the ethical dilemma of the businesswoman trying to be a Christian and a good businesswoman at the same time, the flush of joy at falling in love or welcoming the first child, the frustration of the minorities as well as the white, middle-class backlash. The fabric of the sermon will, like the fabric of the Bible, reflect the actual world in which we live—all of it!

There may be a false impression gained from the emphasis in chapter 7 that because the primary human need to which preaching is addressed today is that of anxiety and hopelessness, preaching is addressed solely to the "private sector" of the individual's life. The fabric of the sermon should make it unmistakably clear that the private sector is totally immersed in the public sector of which each individual is a part: the public world of politics, race relations, corporations, labor unions, and other power structures. If I as a listener seek assurance in the face of a world of frighteningly rapid change, if I need that ultimate security which will enable me to become free for change in the assurance that comes through the retelling of the biblical story that God *is*, and that the God who *is* loves me in all my anxiety and disillusionment, then that security and assurance must come to me as it came through the texture of the biblical witness: not as an escape from the world, but rather in engagement with the world in all its challenges, terrors, joys, and perplexities—all of this so that what is heard on Sunday morning will also make some sense on Sunday afternoon, to say nothing of Monday morning.

This point is frequently rejected by preachers on the basis that people want to get away on Sunday morning from the headlines and the world that baffles them. Of course they do! But the biblical story does not offer an escape from the world. It is precisely *in* the world that God comes to us and seeks response. The fabric of the sermon should make this crystal clear in its secularity.

This does not mean that we can give up specific biblical words and images, of course, for they are the "coinage of the church," the link between what happened then and what is happening now. Hendrik Kraemer calls this "thesaurus" the church's "impregnable rock." But this biblical and theological thesaurus must undergo incessant translation to help a biblically illiterate people understand that words like sin, redemption, reconciliation, grace, and forgiveness are but symbols of fundamental and secular life situations of every person in every age.

And this is precisely where the preacher prays and sweats and prays some more—and all in vain unless the preacher's self-identification with the people in *their* world is so thorough-going that both their present situation and the possibilities open to them through the gospel are reflected with sensitivity and some degree of accuracy.

Meanwhile the problems of translation abound. What shall we do with the *Weltbild* of the Bible which seems so alien to the urban-oriented and science-oriented person of today? As Kraemer indicates, "There is particularly among the majority of lay members of the church a feeling of helplessness in regard to the Bible. . . . It sounds so distant from their ordinary ways of thinking."[6] And so it is with its demons and dead-raisings, its blood sacrifices, its miracles of healing and exorcising, its visions and dreams and theophanies, to say nothing of the dominant images drawn from a rural society of two thousand years ago: shepherds and stewards and vineyards and seed sowers. What can it all possibly mean to a person born and raised in an urban and technological society? The hermeneutical problems are endless. But hermeneutics is precisely the business of the preacher. The preacher can call upon scholarly help from Barth, Bultmann, Ebeling, Fuchs, Moltmann, and the rest. But the task is essentially the preacher's, not the scholar's. The scholar's work exists but to serve the preacher's hours of agony in the struggle to find the meaning behind the meaning and then express the inner meaning in terms of the world in which the preacher and listeners live today.

It is strange, isn't it, if in the exegetical task we take great pains to ascertain the precise authorship, date, and concrete *Sitz im Leben* of a text (and the greater the precision, the more accurate the exegesis), and then are content to relate the text to the present time only in generalities and abstractions. One New Testament scholar has called the exegetical process the "exegetical circle," and the circle is not complete until the text is related to the present situation with the same precision and concreteness with which we ascertained its original historical meaning.

I was a great admirer of the sermons of the great Scottish preacher James Stewart in my earlier years until it dawned on me that his published sermons were originally written and delivered in the context of World War II. Yet one could not even guess the context from reading the sermons. They were and are "timeless sermons," addressed solely to the private sector of the individual's life.

But the timeless sermon, the sermon which could be preached a hundred years ago as well as today, is a poor sermon. Some of the problems in such preaching are suggested in chapter 6. As Helmut Thielicke points out, "It is true . . . that we sometimes hear sermons today which might have been preached in 1880. But this seeming timelessness indicates not an excellence but rather a degeneration of preaching."[7] For if sermons are to be biblical in the deepest sense, they will convey the truth in terms of the now. They will be secular, of this age, in every respect.

The transition to sermons of this kind will take some doing in those congregations for whom biblical preaching has come to mean sermons which steer clear of any allusions to the political, economic, and social realities of their communities. They need to be reintroduced to the reality of the fabric of the biblical witness, which is secular through and through.

If the sermon is to be biblical, the fabric will not only be secular but also dialogical. As Wilder indicates, "The character of religion as it appears in both Old and New Testaments makes the dialogue an inevitable form of rhetorical expression. God is known as one who speaks, addresses, calls, initiates agreements or covenants, engages in public trial scenes, as well as one who invites to mutual converse and understanding."[8] This characteristic of Christian communication, although vitally important, is hardly new and we need not discuss it at length. H. H. Farmer's *The Servant of the Word*, building on Buber's "I-Thou," contains a systematic presentation of what the dialogical approach can mean for preaching.[9] So Hendrik Kraemer: "In the Bible, language means *dialogue*. In the first place, dialogue between God and man. And . . . if this divine-human dialogue is broken or distorted, the dialogue between man and man is in disorder."[10] All we need to recall here is that the dialogue need not be restricted to any particular method of communication. Reuel Howe has made the point: "Any method of communication may be the servant of the dialogical principle. A monological method can be an effective instrument of the dialogical principle."[11]

The trouble with much preaching today is that it is not biblical in the sense of being dialogical. It may start with a text, its formal exegesis may be impeccable, the theology informing the sermon may be apparently faultless, and it may even be punctuated by the phrase,

"But some of you may be asking . . ."—and yet utterly fail as biblical dialogue because the questions assumed are not the questions actually being asked by the people listening, or because the questions are phrased in terms the people would not possibly use, or because the person asking the questions in the sermon may be a straw person with whom no one in the congregation can identify.

If for example the sermon is based on the Lucan version of the story of blind Bartimaeus (Luke 18:35-43), there is an obvious dialogue going on between Jesus and the blind man. But there is also an implicit dialogue going on between Jesus and his disciples who were "blind" to the meaning of the coming passion and death announced immediately before the incident of the healing (Luke 18:31-34). In the sermon identification is set up between the blind man and the "blind" disciples on the one hand, and between the congregation and the preacher on the other. It is crucial that the sermon identify the blindness of the preacher with the blindness of the congregation. Otherwise a dialogue may be taking place between the preacher and the congregation rather than between the preacher-congregation and the Word of God.

A superb example of biblical dialogue in a sermon based on the story of Cain and Abel can be seen in B. Davie Napier's treatment of "the brothers" in *Come Sweet Death* (see above, chap. 7). Napier uses the rhetorical device of the first person singular to set up both his identification with the listeners and to create an actual dialogue between preacher-congregation and the Word of God.

Reuel Howe is exceedingly helpful in this whole area of dialogue, not only in *The Miracle of Dialogue* but also in his *Partners in Preaching.*[12]

The key to authentic dialogue rests largely on the sensitivity of the person in the pulpit, along with the possibility of lay participation in the preparation of the sermon to help insure the presence of genuine dialogue in the sermon. The point to be made here is that the biblical character of speech requires that the fabric of the sermon be dialogical. And the dialogical language of the Bible is, not surprisingly, the kind of language which will get a hearing today when the air is electric with questions.

If, then, the fabric of the sermon will reflect the biblical characteristics of secularity and dialogue, a third characteristic of biblical rhetoric will be that it takes the form of a story told, as a whole and in its parts. It is a history. It is not strange that this is so because, to come back to Wilder again, "all life has the character of a story and a plot."[13]

In the first place, the dramatic form of a biblical address will affect the structure of the sermon. Each sermon should have something of the dramatic form of a play or short story: tightly knit, one part leading into and dependent upon the next, with some possibility of suspense and surprise evident in the development and at the end. This is in contrast to the classic "three-point sermon" which all too frequently turns out to be three independent statements developed at some length with some relationship to a central theme (for example the three marks of a Christian: faith, hope, and love. It is textual, theologically sound, but essentially unbiblical unless the three are woven in some way into a plot or story.) The legacy of the nineteenth-century pulpit, with its characteristic announcement of the theme at the beginning of the sermon along with the major divisions or heads, has laid a dreary hand on much of the preaching still done today. (See in contrast the illustrative sermons included in this volume.)

If a sermon is to be biblical at its deepest level, it will draw us into the development of a plot or story, the end of which is still in doubt. I know that the suspense may be difficult to achieve, since everyone knows that the preacher is against sin and for God. And yet there are possibilities of suspense even in a situation where the cards are heavily stacked against it. For example Martin Marty suggests that the effectiveness of a sermon might well be judged by the reaction "I never thought of it in quite that way before" rather than by the effusive cliché that it was a "very inspiring message."

Suppose for example you wish to preach a "teaching sermon" on the meaning of the biblical word *glory*. You may take for a text John 13:31, "Now is the Son of man glorified." In the interest of suspense, you do not begin with the text but rather with a reflection of what the word glory suggests to the listeners. So images of the accepted meaning of glory are rehearsed: an angel chorus in the night sky over Bethlehem, the stars and stripes waving in the breeze—Old Glory—the glory of a sunset, and so on. Then in contrast you introduce the text, spoken on the night before Christ died. Then you might end with the image of Martin Luther King lying in a pool of blood on the porch of a second-rate hotel in Memphis. The glory of God? There is enough suspense and surprise in the biblical record to infuse our sermons with some of the elements of suspense and surprise.

Moreover, as Wilder suggests, in the biblical stories the hearer or reader "finds himself in the middle of the action. We are in the middle of the play."[14] The last word is not in the sermon; it is still to be spoken.

Closely allied to the dramatic story-form of the sermon is the fact that the biblical story is told chiefly in the indicative mood, the basic mood in which any story is told. To be sure, the Bible includes exhortation and command. And doubtless sermons preached from New Testament times on down to the present have reflected the hortatory and imperative aspects of biblical address. But the basic fabric of the Bible is in the indicative. It is reportorial. And I suspect that the preaching that will contribute most to the renewal of your people will reflect this emphasis upon the indicative. So Harvey Cox: "Because [the church] as the avant-garde announces the coming of a new era which has already begun but is not yet complete [We are in the middle of the play!], its message is in the indicative mood, not the imperative. It does not urge or exhort people. It simply makes known what has happened, that 'the acceptable year of the Lord' has arrived."[15]

What, then, becomes of the familiar homiletical advice that we should "preach for a verdict." We do. But we don't use the high-pressure hard sell with a person who is callous from listening day in and day out to the high-pressure hard sell. Moreover, many churchgoers have been led to expect a dreary procession of musts, oughts, and shoulds which bounce off their hides like hailstones on concrete.

In preaching for a verdict in the indicative mood, furthermore, we respect the freedom of the individual to accept or reject. If we really believe that the response of a person to the hearing of the gospel is the promised work of the Holy Spirit, then we shall take that promise in all seriousness. Report the facts of life *sub specie eternitatis* as accurately, factually, and imaginatively as possible, then let the Holy Spirit and the listener work it out from there. Was this not the method of our Lord? Jesus, the consummate preacher for our age as well as for his, would begin, "The kingdom of heaven is like . . ." and then would follow a crisp, tightly structured, secular narrative with the issue of it all left in the lap or in the ears of the listener: "He that hath ears to hear, let him hear."

I believe we can win new respect for the pulpit as a valid form of communicating the gospel if its fabric reflects the fabric of the Bible in its low-keyed, dramatic form, which leaves the issue in the air rather than pushing a person into a corner—whether by exhortation, demand, or purple rhetoric—and pushing for a verdict. W. H. Auden reminds us that

> . . . truth, like love and sleep, resents
> Approaches that are too intense.[16]

Finally, the fabric of the sermon will be as lean and spare as the fabric of the Bible. The fact that the Bible is often studied as great literature is due in no small part to the way in which the biblical stories are told: no wordiness, no superfluity of adjectives, but lean and spare, the narrative making its point briefly and sharply. From the great stories of the Old Testament, Abraham, Jacob, Jonah, to the parables of Jesus and the pericopes of the gospels, the fabric is that of stories told crisply, sometimes rough-hewn, always quickly and surely to the point. Because life is not wordy. It may be complex, paradoxical, baffling, like the story of Abraham commanded to sacrifice the child of promise, but it is not prolix.

The fact that the sermon will be lean and spare will force us to cut and trim the words we use, the juicy adjectives, the fancy alliterations, the quoting of hymns and of sentimental religious poetry, and the abstractions—especially the abstractions. This last is no small problem since all the cardinal points in the biblical drama have come down to us in verbal symbols in the form of abstract nouns—creation, incarnation, redemption, forgiveness, resurrection—words from which the blood of action has been drained. Every time we use one of these abstractions, and even such concrete nouns as sin and grace and gospel which through overuse have also become abstractions, two things happen. First, we rely upon the listener to substitute for the abstraction a concrete picture of the action, and this, in the course of oral speech, has to be virtually instantaneous. Second, we rely upon the listener to substitute for the abstract symbol the same picture of concrete action which is in the mind of the preacher. Taken together, these make the use of abstractions a risky business.

The same thing is true of the use of generalizations which are abstracted from specifics (if they are honest!). In preaching, as in the biblical record, the preacher learns to use specifics in place of or in addition to the generalization. Preachers will learn to ask themselves, when tempted to use a generalization, "What, specifically, do you have in mind?" When for example they call for their congregations to "witness to the world in the home, in the office, at school, or in the street," preachers will ask themselves, "What, specifically, do you have in mind?"

Preachers need to remind themselves constantly that God comes to us not in abstractions or generalizations but in the concrete give-and-take of actual life. To be sure, we will use abstractions on occasion because they are part of the biblical thesaurus, but every time we use one bare and unadorned it is a calculated risk. Better by far that the sermon reflect the blood and soil of actual life.

Obviously it takes more words to picture in vivid action, even by suggestion and concrete allusion, the meaning of forgiveness or sanctification than it does to use the shorthand of abstraction. But some things are inevitably left to the imagination of the hearer, and it is safer and more biblical to let a listener's mind work over what is suggested through concrete narrative, allusion, or illustration than through the use of abstraction.

Martin Marty, in discussing the use of the mass media for the communication of the Christian faith, has a sentence which is helpful for the preacher: "The communication known as presentation has a promissory character; it tends to tantalize and to offer more than it can deliver, but what it offers can be honest."[17]

Where abstractions, then, tend to stifle or preclude further consideration, presentation—as narrative, allusion, suggestion—invites and intrigues. It respects the listeners' freedom to make up their own minds, and at the same time invites them to participate in other structures of the church's life where there can be fuller opportunity for discussion, dialogue, and debate.

So the fabric of the sermon, by reflecting more faithfully the fabric of the biblical source of its message in its secularity, its dialogical character, its dramatic story-form in the indicative mood, and its lean and spare style, may speak to the person come of age in terms which will give the gospel a hearing at least, even if in their freedom some persons may well reject it. But what more are we called to do as preachers if not to preach for a verdict?

NOTES

1. Amos N. Wilder, *The Language of the Gospel: Early Christian Rhetoric* (New York: Harper & Row, Publishers, 1964), pp. 10, 12–13.

2. Martin E. Marty, *Improper Opinion* (Philadelphia: Westminster Press, 1961), p. 105.

3. Wilder, *Language of the Gospel*, p. 82.

4. Gerhard Ebeling, *Word and Faith* (Philadelphia: Fortress Press, 1963), p. 359.

5. Hendrik Kraemer, *The Communication of the Christian Faith* (Philadelphia: Westminster Press, 1956), pp. 124–25.

6. Ibid., p. 93.

7. Helmut Thielicke, *The Trouble with the Church,* trans. John W. Doberstein (Grand Rapids: Baker Book House, 1978), p. 98.

8. Wilder, *Language of the Gospel*, p. 52.

9. H. H. Farmer, *The Servant of the Word* (Philadelphia: Fortress Press, 1964).

10. Kraemer, *Communication of the Christian Faith,* p. 65.

11. Reuel Howe, *The Miracle of Dialogue* (New York: Seabury Press, 1963), p. 40.

12. Ibid.; see also idem, *Partners in Preaching* (New York: Seabury Press, 1967).

13. Wilder, *Language of the Gospel,* p. 64.

14. Ibid., p. 67.

15. Harvey Cox, *The Secular City* (New York: Macmillan Publishing Co., 1965), pp. 130–31.

16. Quoted in Robert E. C. Browne, *The Ministry of the Word* (Philadelphia: Fortress Press, 1976), p. 116.

17. Martin E. Marty, *Second Chance for American Protestants* (New York: Harper & Row, Publishers, 1963), p. 4.

SERMON:

Disturbed by Joy

Edmund A. Steimle

At the conclusion of a three-hour service on Good Friday the host minister bade me goodbye: "I hope you have a blessed Easter." It was a natural thing to say. I think it was not just pious language; I think he meant it. And so do others who say it in more conventional terms: "Have a happy Easter." For this is the normal expectation for this day of days, isn't it so? That it will be marked by joy. This is its dominant mood: the joyful celebration of victory over the suffering and death and darkness of Good Friday.

But it's a strange circumstance that in the narrative accounts of the resurrection, joy was not the initial reaction. The initial reaction was one of embarrassment, of fear, of awe.

I know it is always a ticklish business to attempt to get back of the Easter message itself—"That Christ died . . . that he was buried and that he was raised on the third day . . ."—and attempt to discover what actually happened through a study of the resurrection narratives. It's ticklish because even the least scholarly among us can recognize through the most casual reading of the narratives in the four Gospels that they do not agree in detail as to how this experience of Christ alive first came, or even as to where.

Furthermore, it is generally acknowledged that the narratives which describe the resurrection appearances are considerably later than the

[Edmund A. Steimle, *Disturbed by Joy* (Philadelphia: Fortress Press, 1967). This sermon originally appeared in the March 1965 issue of the *Union Seminary Quarterly Review* and is used by permission.]

record of the content of the message itself. And as scholars suggest, the narratives may well be embroidered by legendary additions.

And yet granting all this, it is still a curious fact that in all four accounts it is clear that the immediate impact of the experience of Christ alive is not joy, as we might well expect. Rather it is an experience of embarrassment, of fear, almost of terror. So the New English Bible in its translation of the Easter narratives uses words like terrified, dumbfounded, beside themselves with terror, falling prostrate before him. Even Günther Bornkamm, who comes right out and says that the story of the women at the tomb in Mark is "obviously a legend," nevertheless exclaims, "[But see] how his story is told! The wonderful event of the resurrection is not even depicted, such is the reticence and awe."[1] And when you come to the account in the Gospel of John, in its way it is even more reticent. It says simply, "they did not recognize him."

Now all this adds up to the fact that whatever else the disciples and followers of Jesus may have hoped for, desired, anticipated, prior to the death and after it, quite unlike our attitude today, they did not expect this! This, apparently, was the last thing they expected. They were embarrassed, frightened, confused, awestruck. And it seems to me, if we are to recapture the authentic message of Easter, its substance, we have to come to terms with this strange reaction.

And yet admittedly it is all but impossible for us to recapture the same mood of embarrassment and fright. Easter is hardly surprising or embarrassing for most of us. All through Lent and Holy Week and Good Friday we anticipate its joy—as we should! We'd be playing a morbid game of charades if we didn't. And so each year we anticipate reliving the joy that it brings. Even now we look forward to the next Easter, hoping that it will be late. Because despite the obvious distortions of the resurrection message in the analogy of the renewal of nature in the spring, we've come to expect nature to join in the joyous celebration. The crocus and the daffodil ought to be nodding their silent hallelujahs too. But in all of this annual anticipation, this looking forward to the expected joys of Easter, something tends to drop out of our understanding of the substance of the Easter message.

Moreover, this lack of embarrassment and surprise is fed by the old Platonic notion of the immortality of the soul. We know that it is theologically disreputable these days to assume that there is some indestructible inner core inside of us which death cannot touch, which makes its claim on God to see to it that when we die we really don't. But it's difficult to shake off. We may reject it with our minds, but we've taken it in with our mother's milk, our culture is filled with hints of it, it dies hard. Yet as long as it persists there's not much embarrassment when Easter rolls around with its announcement that what we've felt all along to be true is now given its annual Christian sanction. Death cannot be the end, Easter or no Easter.

But if all our normal expectations regarding Easter undercut and contradict this strange reaction of embarrassment and fear on that first Easter morning, a radically different mood works powerfully against it too. And that is the prevailing mood that the resurrection as a happy ending spoils the whole story, that the drama of Jesus would be far stronger and make a far greater appeal to this post-Christian age without all this supernatural clap-trap brought in at the end with a dead man suddenly brought back to life again. Wouldn't the story of Jesus of Nazareth be more powerful and truer to itself in being less self-centered, if his life had ended in death? How much more courageous were he to give his life in obedient trust to the God who made him and gave him his mission without this "reward" tacked on at the end. Some people say they'll take their Christianity straight, thank you, without any Hollywood ending which leaves everyone living happily ever after.

It's an understandable reaction, this mood which rejects the resurrection stories as pious fiction. The only trouble with it, apart from the fact that it denies the sum and substance of the earliest Christian records we have, is that it disregards entirely this strange reaction in the Easter narratives. When they experienced Christ alive they didn't go walking off hand in hand into the sunset with a choir of angels singing softly in the wings, "There is a happy land . . ." On the contrary, "They were terrified . . . dumbfounded . . . ran away beside themselves with terror."

Although it is impossible for us to recapture this mood after all the years, perhaps if we can come to some understanding of what lay behind it and why it persists in all the resurrection narratives, it may give added depth to our appreciation of the substance of the Easter message, that Christ died and rose again.

For what it means, to begin with, is that we cannot escape God—

even in death. May not the resistance to the miracle of the resurrection uncover a deep-seated desire not to let go of my hold on life—even in death? For if death is the end, if there is nothing more, then I through my mortal body rotting in the grave have the last word, not God. Then God and his ways, which are not *our* ways, are made to coincide with my understanding of courage and faithfulness and reward. For all the honesty evident in the refusal to accept the miraculous, the supernatural here at the end of Christ's life, is there not embedded in that honest reluctance a trace at least of the pride of the creature who insists on determining life's ultimate destiny rather than leaving the issue to God? I will trust God in life here and now, give myself wholly to his will of love here and now, even grant him the power to bring about a new life—a "new being"—here and now, but I will not grant him power over my death.

But beyond that, does not the resurrection mean that we cannot escape the startling ways in which God acts? Obviously the disciples, the women, the followers of Jesus were distraught and disillusioned in the face of his death. They wept at the cross and on the way to the tomb. But they had accepted it. They had come to terms with it. "They went with their spices to anoint him." How that little detail underlines how quickly they learned to accept Christ's death and live with it. For does not all life end so? You and I quickly learn to come to terms with grief and disillusionment and death. We learn to live with it. We have to.

So was not part of their astonishment and embarrassment and fear the sudden realization that God would act *through* suffering and disillusionment and death? To be sure, they'd had their hopes, their dreams, all the promises of life abundant which he had held out to them. But never in their wildest moments had they considered the possibility that God would accomplish his vast purpose of love *through* death and suffering and disillusionment. It's one thing to come to terms with death and disillusionment, to live with it and accept it. We all have to do that. It's quite another to be faced with the reality that this is how God acts, how he works out his purposes for the world. No wonder they were dumbfounded and terrified. For now they knew. God does not save us from suffering and death; he saves us through it. "Take up your cross and follow me" was no longer a possibility to be held at arm's length as a conceivable course of action alongside some others perhaps less stringent. Now it was there, living before their eyes. Life—abundant life—is not cheap.

And that brings us to this: before Easter brings its inevitable joy, it brings judgment. And no doubt that's what terrified them too. For as they buried him in the tomb, they buried not only their hopes and dreams and all the promises he had held out to them, all the love and care he had shown, all his concern for the unlovely and downtrodden— all this was buried with him. But this was not all that was buried. Along with all this they also buried their shoddy faith, their shabby quarrels as to who was to be greatest in the kingdom, all the petty jealousies and impatience with him, the ugly scenes of denial and betrayal—all this was buried with him too. And in that burial, as Tillich has reminded us, is the powerful symbol of being forgotten.[2] As they buried him, they also buried the fact that they all forsook him and fled in the not unreasonable hope that that unpleasantness would soon be forgotten too.

No wonder they were "beside themselves with terror" on that first resurrection morning. For all of this was now alive again! The promises, the love, the vibrant life they had known, to be sure, but all the sad betrayals and shabby pettiness and indifference too. It had all come back! For there is no forgetting. Now it is all alive again. "And they were afraid." Is it surprising? Death was no longer a forgetting; it was a remembering.

And so the most characteristic initial word on Easter is not "Be of good cheer" but "Be not afraid." For the one who returns, who brings it all back to life again, who permits no escape into death, who allows no burial, no forgetting, is the one we know. And with recognition, the fear, the embarrassment, turns into joy: "Then were the disciples glad when they saw the Lord." For now despite the judgment, the bringing alive of all he had been and of all they had been, they knew they could trust that the judgment he brought alive was the judgment of love. So Easter becomes a commentary on John's words "There is no fear in love, for perfect love casteth out fear."

Now is this gladness, this joy, possible until the last enemy, death, has actually been overcome? Not just for ourselves but for others? There are those who say, as one college chaplain said to me not long ago, that the meaning of Easter is primarily the reality of the new life Christ brings here and now; what happens to us afterward is secondary. And there's much to be said for that, of course. For it's true, what God has to offer to us now through the life, death, and resurrection of Christ is the conquest of all life's enemies in the world around us: the injustice and prejudice and indifference and fascination with ourselves, the anxieties and resulting pride and self-justification. All of these enemies of life here and now are overcome in the reconciling love of God in Christ. We don't have to run around like scared rabbits—or perhaps more accurately, like frightened hyenas—bolstering our little insecurities by feeding on the lives of those around us. Life—abundant life—is a possibility for us here and now. All the doors that shut us in here and now, fear and estrangement and hostility, all of these are overcome. The doors are opened to abundant life.

But if death, the last enemy, is not destroyed, the last door not opened, then what is life's issue? Fertilizer for the generations to come? To be sure, Medgar Evers, the little Negro children in Sunday school, and the rest of the martyrs in the civil rights struggle have provided powerful fertilizer not only for sermons but for the civil rights movement. But is the last door, the door that banged shut on them—death—to remain shut? The door which says no to all life's ultimate hopes and dreams?

I can understand a man saying that so far as he's concerned it makes no difference. The door can remain shut since there's so much in life to be realized here and now. But is this not in the end at least tainted with a self-centered view? What of the thousands upon thousands of people who have known nothing but closing doors in life here and now—the mentally defective, the deformed children, the warped and twisted minds and bodies that know little if anything in this world but doors banging shut in their faces from childhood on until the last door, the last enemy, bangs shut? What about them? Defective fertilizer, perhaps?

T. S. Eliot puts a haunting line into the mouth of one of the Magi coming to seek the child born in Bethlehem:

> . . . were we led all that way
> for Birth or Death? . . .[3]

No, says Paul. All of life's enemies, including the last enemy, are overcome. "For he must reign until he has put all his enemies under his feet. The last enemy to be destroyed is death. . . . Death is swallowed up in victory.''

So the Easter cycle: from death and grief and disillusionment, through embarrassment, fear, and even terror, to the joy that is its ultimate and predominant mood. For God's yes will not abide life's no or death's no. "Thanks be to God who giveth us the victory through our Lord Jesus Christ.''

NOTES

1. Günther Bornkamm, *Jesus of Nazareth* (New York: Harper & Row, Publishers, 1960), p. 183.

2. Paul Tillich, *The Eternal Now* (New York: Charles Scribner's Sons, 1963), p. 33.

3. T. S. Eliot, "Journey of the Magi," *Collected Poems, 1909–1962* (New York: Harcourt, Brace & World, 1963), p. 69. Used by permission.

PART FIVE

LEARNING TO PREACH

11

Homiletics in a New Context

Ardith Spierling Hayes

Dialogue between men and women is the new context for the teaching of homiletics. One woman, when asked to respond to this new fact, replied rather tartly but with logic, "Women learn to preach the same way that men learn to preach." On one level that expresses the truth of the matter. On another level it expresses what is now a realizable possibility.

Feminist theologians and biblical scholars have, from their perspective as women, raised issues which are particularly relevant to the homiletical and hermeneutical tasks. The homiletics teacher has the opportunity to enable students to identify and learn from these issues by raising them to the level of awareness so that they become part of the educational content. In what follows we shall attend to some of these emerging issues: imagery, language, authority, and symbols. Moreover, students need to examine the dynamics in the formation of religious consciousness to which these issues give rise, and we shall also be discussing some of these processes in the course of this chapter. Women and men together can examine their assumptions, share their experiences, and articulate their perceptions. The resulting dialogue will be critical—and sometimes threatening—as it moves toward the shaping of a faithful human response and witness to the Word.

All preachers must deal with the problem of speaking about a God of whom we are forbidden to make any image. Our main source of help is the Bible with its rich variety of images which help us to understand what God is like. Images are especially powerful because they are understood as participating in some way in the reality of that which they represent. The issue for women is how these images are used. Frequently what begins as a valid theological insight is used selectively. Women question for instance whether using the dominant image of God as divine patriarch has not led us into limiting, hurtful, and sometimes false notions of who we are, and of what we are to do, in relationship to this God. It may have been inevitable that male clergy would come to be seen as direct representations of God the male patriarch, but men have cooperated willingly in being hung with this image.

Mary Daly in her book *Beyond God the Father* identifies three false notions of deity which, as she says, "still haunt the prayers, hymns, sermons, and religious education of Christianity."[1] One is the "God of explanation," God as the justifier of the way things are. The way things are has tended to include the notion of a male-defined and male-dominated social order. Another is the "God of otherworldliness," who rewards and punishes after death. This notion of God has been used to reinforce submission to all sorts of deprivation in this life as well as to questionably derived standards of behavior. Women are among the groups who have suffered most from this use of religious authority. Daly's third false deity is the "Judge of sin," whose main function is to confirm the rightness of the rules and regulations of the prevailing system. Through *misuse* of this notion of God, women have been encouraged in self-destructive guilt and taught that when things go wrong in their primary relationships, it is somehow their fault. An extreme example of this kind of thinking is the prevalent phenomenon of battered women who can be helped only after they are relieved of the notion that they are somehow to blame for their condition.

This too-rapid survey of the problems clustering around one especially prevalent image of God does not do justice to the range and depth of Daly's treatment of the subject. It is meant to be illustrative of a problem which is of particular concern to women—the way we use images, even those which may express a theological truth. The problem invites indulgence in the human tendency to make projections, an indulgence that results in unexamined projections onto God of the human traits that are socially and culturally reinforced as the dominant or desirable ones. No responsible preacher wishes to instill in the congregation an image of a God limited by our projections. The point is that we cannot adequately examine our projections, conscious and unconscious, using only one lens, that of male experience. The classroom affords the opportunity to fully include in the critique of our images the contributions women can make. There are truths to which women can point because they have had the experience of being on the receiving end of some very inadequate projections; there are also some truths they can share out of their growing sense of female equality of experience.

There is no desire to replace a false patriarchal deity with an equally false matriarchal deity, nor is there any desire to have a sort of "both-and" image of God. The latter has often resulted in a schizophrenic image of God, the product of combining a romanticized feminine with a macho masculine to produce what Daly calls the "Godfather image," the "marriage of tenderness and violence" so intricately blended in the patriarchal ideal."[2] The task for all of us who grapple with the issue is to take the measure of our combined human experience and examine it in the light of the Bible's witness to a God who is imageless, yet in whose image both men and women are created.

The remaining issues to be discussed—issues of language, authority, and symbols—derive in large part from the kinds of images we use for God. The so-called language issue has generated more heat than light and is often dismissed by belittling it or by labeling it as outrageous. A responsible teacher can no longer ignore or dismiss it in this way but rather must raise it intentionally as a serious issue for inclusion in the curriculum.

It was not until I heard a preacher speak of a woman's self-understanding as being that of a "daughter of God" that I grasped intuitively the immediacy with which God confronts me. I had no idea that as long as I could hide behind a hazy notion of myself as some kind of "son of God," I was avoiding full responsibility for myself in the sight of God. As a daughter of God I found I could own and affirm my female being and that I was called to stop the self-deprecation and the excuses to which it formerly gave rise. Not long after that experience, I began to pray to God as mother as well as father and discovered I felt known by God more fully than I ever had. This taking away of the hiding place and of the excuse for dependence upon male intermediaries may be one reason many women still resist the use of inclusive language in worship.

The power with which masculine language has determined our perceptions and experience of God is illustrated in the angry, often frantic resistance to changing it. The extent to which language change threatens some men is the clearest rebuttal to the commonly used argument that masculine terms are generic and include everyone. I recall the emotionally heated attack made by a male pastor on a United Presbyterian General Assembly resolution concerning language. It called upon the seminaries to study the language issue, to make occasion for theologians to address students on this issue, and to provide for the students experiences in inclusive language worship. This particular pastor wanted the committee upon which we were serving to try to have the resolution stopped, because, as he said, "this is only the opening round in a movement to eliminate all the traditional ways in which we speak of God that are so important to our people. There will come a day when we can no longer speak of God our Father, or Jesus Christ his Son, and the very meaning of the Christian faith will be taken away from our people." The debate continued, and after listening a while longer I said to him, "It sounds like you want us to have the United Presbyterian Church take a stand for the maleness of God."

"That's right," he said.

In facing up to the language issue, we need to work with both the theological limitations of our personal images of God and with the pain of outgrowing them. For men, part of this pain comes from the fact that traditional worship has encouraged them to identify their personal worth with masculine images for God and to equate God's nearness to them with the masculine language of the traditional liturgy. I believe that part of this pain, however, for men as well as for women, arises from the same phenomenon I experienced once I understood myself as a daughter of God. It is the pain of giving up old dependencies, whatever form they take, and acknowledging that one stands personally accountable before the God of all. Our use of language has tended to mask this for men and for women: for men by implying a false security (they participate in the rightness of things by virtue of their gender); for women by implying a false exclusion (they are excused by virtue of gender and participate only indirectly).

Authority is another issue which, like language, needs fresh assessment. The traditional accoutrements of preaching have reinforced an image of patriarchal authority which appears to define the pulpit as a male preserve. In many periods of our history this image coincided well with authority as understood and exercised in the social and political structures. Interestingly, it is precisely the authority of the preacher which causes women the greatest difficulty in imagining themselves in that role. Men and women alike have experienced unhelpful and constricting preaching which mistakes the authority of the preacher for the authoritarianism of a threatened moralist. Nevertheless, men whose goal in ministry goes far beyond the wooden authoritarianism of that kind of preacher are able more comfortably to imagine themselves in the role of preacher. For one thing, they have had role models who are like themselves male. For another, they grow up accustomed to the idea of exercising authority.

Dialogue with women in the classroom affords the occasion for all homiletics students to reexamine their understanding of what constitutes the authority of the preacher. I suggest that the issue is most helpfully redefined as an issue not of authority but of authenticity. Authentic preaching does not presume to pronounce upon your experience without having honestly examined and shared mine. The prophetic tradition, which we think of as a primary example of the authority of the preacher, grew from the anguished struggles of individuals, people of sensitive conscience and uncompromising faith, with the authenticity of a God whose very being was known in the carrying out of the divine purpose. The authority of God was understood to be the authority of action in the sphere of human lives and history. The authority of the preacher is carried in the weight of authentic witness to the divine inevitability as it is perceived and experienced. The heavier the message, the more anguished and personal the struggle which gave rise to it. The more joyful the news and profound the hope, the more deeply has the preacher drunk of that joy and sounded the depths of that hope.

Theological and ecclesiastical tradition have also shaped our understanding of authority in preaching. In some cases the ecclesiastical commissioning or ordering still denies to women the authority to preach. In all of our religious traditions the relationship between the personal, individual conviction of calling or vocation and the institutional authentification of that calling is an area for continuing examination and consideration. This must be so, for the witness of the preacher always has a context, the community of faith as a particular expression of the body of Christ. In the history of every tradition there are examples of individuals whose inner convictions were so compelling that they challenged the institutional order and sometimes were the catalysts for changing it. Discovering the stories of women and men who precipitated issues of authenticity and authority is both fun and inspiring. Their stories illuminate our struggle with these issues today.

Religious symbols are yet another area for examination by a homiletics class. Inevitably symbols take on attributes of the human beings for whom they are invested with meaning. Our religious symbols have tended to derive from—and reinforce ambivalence and divisions within—our images for God, and usually to split along lines of gender difference. One thinks of the familiar lament by women that the major biblical symbolism of woman as temptress, virgin, and mother has been emphasized to the exclusion of woman as prophet, teacher, minister, judge, and wisdom figure. Feminists in the church today are reclaiming the "lost" female religious symbols—the divine mother; the nurturing goddess of earth, of cycles, and of harvest; the traditions of prophetess and wise woman. This reclamation is very enlivening because it enables the discovery that woman have equal access with men to the roots of religious consciousness.

However, we will go badly astray theologically if we settle for a separate but equal symbolism—so many for your side, so many for ours! Such a division encourages projection of those parts of ourselves which are lost to us—or which we have perceived and rejected—onto another. Men and women have been dehumanized as they have been falsely masculinized or falsely feminized. The notion that woman is especially close to nature has resulted in her bearing the blame for man's alienation from it and the burden for his reconciliation to it. Mother's Day sermons usually manage to imply that the ideal woman is chaste, if not celibate most of the time, yet romantically alluring so as to bring out the "higher nature" of her husband and children, keeping them enthralled and close to home. She is the guardian of all those values of thrift, hard work, sobriety, and duty which are the foundation of any capitalist society; yet since she is also the weaker sex she is in danger of a disastrous fall from grace should she forsake the dependency to which she has been so graciously sentenced. Women have, conversely, burdened men with overwhelming responsibility to be the initiators and implementers in most areas of their common life. It is a sin against God, in whose image a woman has been created, for her to make another the repository of her own lost self.

Salvation is among other things understood to mean wholeness. All of our symbols are corrected and reconciled in the symbol of the cross. The life and teachings of Jesus of Nazareth, the death and resurrection of Christ the incarnate Lord speak most powerfully to all of our issues of image, authority, language, and symbols, and bring them into focus. It is a mistake however to move too quickly to the resolution that is suggested by the marvelous examples found in the way Jesus dealt with women or to focus too superficially on our reconciliation and oneness in Christ. To do so is to duck the hard wrestling with their respective experiences which men and women must do together if their preaching is to mediate the efficacy of that reconciliation to other men and women caught in similar struggles. I remember a bitter experience in a committee of the church that reflected real and ugly racial conflict and was deeply hurtful to several people in the group. When I spoke to the experience at the close of our time together and suggested that we acknowledge our dividedness and pray for the grace to seek reconciliation and forgiveness, one man rose to remind me that I was simply being carried away by feelings. "After all," he said, "we are already one in Christ."

When dealing with the images we use in speaking of God, we are at the same time saying something about the ways in which we have ordered our lives and about our self-understanding as creatures who bear this image. Women and men learning to preach can begin by considering who we are before God and how adequately we express our full selves. Perhaps it is helpful to begin by recognizing some commonalities in our experience. For instance we are at this time citizens sharing in the economic and cultural realities of this historical period. In the same way we are inheritors of a tradition and members of a body of believers who hold in common that particular tradition as well as a mission within the context of the present institutional reality of the church. Consider what accountabilities we hold in relation to our present historical situation. Will anything less than the whole response of human beings who are not divided within themselves or alienated from one another enable us to be faithful—especially as we seek to help members of our congregations understand themselves in the same light of God's purpose for them?

We need to consider the ways in which people avoid affirming their wholeness. Men and women might draw up their own lists of "sins" in this regard and then compare them. Women's sins tend to be those of self-negation, resistance to autonomy, avoidance of accountability, failure either to own the power they have or to use it honestly and openly, retreats into the false feminity which has been foisted on them in fantasy and romanticism, putting down other women, and using men. A class might consider in this regard a common theme in preaching and the probable effect it has on women whose primary sin is self-negation in some form. That theme is the call to self-sacrifice and servanthood. Men's sins against their own wholeness tend to include fear of dependency, fear of loss of control, denial of feelings, dismissing another person's data because they don't conform to their rules, abuse of power, cutting humor, competing with other men, and using women. Preaching which implies, however indirectly, that we must earn our salvation will have the effect of reinforcing all of these sins which are committed in the name of a phony masculine ideal.

Human sexuality is another area in which preachers have an opportunity to help men and women accept and express their wholeness as creatures of God. Institutional religion has never quite managed to welcome the reality of human sexuality or to deal comfortably with it. Christian preaching tends to emphasize the alienation to which it can give rise rather than affirming its rightful inclusion in the wholeness of beings who were created male and female. What men and women have inflicted upon one another because of gender difference would appear to come from a basic dis-ease with our created selves.

If preaching is to be helpful, then women and men in the homiletics class will need to understand, own, and include their sexuality as a strength which they bring to ministry and to preaching. If the authority of the preacher is based in authenticity of witness, then it is seriously compromised if the preacher is not fully the person that she or he is before God and with other people. Women who preach tell rueful stories about those who are able to hear their message only by imagining them to be somehow or other sexless. Neither do men benefit from being considered as somehow above normal human desires. It is hurtful to all of us when we cannot be our full selves.

Students learning to preach can work through some of the texts which impinge most directly upon human sexuality. It would be very interesting to work in groups preparing to preach on Genesis 3. What differences would emerge if one group were all men, another all women, and a third group mixed men and women? Or ask a man and a woman to preach on the story of the woman at the well, as a male colleague and I did on successive Sundays. Then let the class engage them in discussion of the differences in terms of what each was saying both positively and negatively about human sexuality. Or examine the biblical imagery surrounding marriage and the texts most commonly used in connection with marriage, and ask how the same comments upon these texts would be heard by different groups: the single, divorced, gay, teenage, married—man or woman. How do we deal with the fact that a prevalent Old Testament analogy for the bridegroom "taking" a bride is God's possession of the land? The Book of Hosea gives rise to highly educational discussion about the theological integrity of the text in relation to the imagery of harlotry. The point is not to abandon the search for theological integrity but to become much more sensitive to the easy assumptions which have caused male preachers to put women down badly while in the same breath asking them to respond to the good news. Such discussions require a commitment on the part of student and teacher to listen carefully to one another and to accept feedback on how each of them is being heard.

Another approach to the positive inclusion of human sexuality is to examine the many ways in which it affects our self-image, our image of others, and the ways in which others see and hear us. It might be very helpful for women who fear taking on the role of preacher with its implications of authority and responsibility to hear men talk about their own fears in this regard. Such an exchange might provide the means to move from the false issue of how women can reconcile their femininity with such a role to a recognition of the real issue for all of us. How can we accept our sexuality as a part of our wholeness before God, and how through the medium of preaching can we help those in our congregations to do the same?

Working positively with the images we use to express what God is like, and therefore what we are meant to be like, can be fun as men and women search out their favorite masculine and feminine images in the Bible. For example, God is said to be like a father; God is also said to be like a mother. God is said to be a mighty man of war; before him the inhabitants of the earth are as grasshoppers. But this same God nourished a faminished people with milk and honey; was a woman searching for a lost coin; had all the care and patience of a potter at the wheel; and was above all a lover forever reconciling a faithless people back to the encircling arms.

Searching out biblical imagery merges with the task of considering the adequacy of the symbolism we use to express the truth of relationships—social, institutional, and personal. What does the Bible tell us about the city as expression of the reign of God? What does a city look like that does not do violence to the created nature of its male and female citizens? The church is called the body of Christ. What does it mean to express the wholeness of the body in our ecclesiastical structures? In the many masculine and feminine images which describe God and God's activity, what do we learn about human parenthood, about the relationships between co-workers, between lovers, between brothers and sisters? Students can share portions of their stories or critical incidents from their experiences as men and women. The task of the teacher and other students is first to hear accurately and then to join in considering what biblical imagery and symbolism most aptly expresses and/or speaks to the meaning of these stories.

Foremost among the ways in which we learn to deal with the authority issue is the inclusion, for the benefit of both women and men, of female role models. Women especially need this experience, but as men deal with their own reactions to it they may come to understand better where they really are in relation to the authority role of the preacher.

A woman who is a seminary middler recently reported an experience which, as she said, she hoped need not happen ever again to any other woman. She was giving her first sermon. "In the middle of it," she said, "I realized that I was in the congregation watching myself preach. And I was the first woman I'd ever seen preach."

I remember trying to explain to a male colleague the impact on women, clergy and lay, of their first worship experiences under the leadership of a woman minister. "Suppose," I said, "you'd grown up in the church, as most of us have, and your only experiences of ministers were of women in that role. What would it be like the first time you were led in worship by a man?"

"Pretty powerful," he said.

The entire class needs to hear women preachers. The experience should be followed by discussion of students' reactions, feelings, and responses, possibly including the preacher herself in the discussion.

This should not be a onetime experience, for women's styles and approaches to preaching vary as widely as do those of men.

Homiletics professors are still predominantly men. They and the students will be helped greatly to deal with gender issues if some team teaching is done with women. A female colleague from another department in the seminary or a woman pastor from the area could be invited to team teach for a carefully planned segment of the course or for the entire term. Team teaching takes more time, as we all know, but given the general state of unpreparedness in the church for the entrance of women into the pastorate, this may be some of the most valuable time we could spend at this point in our history.

As we work through the issues of authority/authenticity we come naturally into a collegial style of functioning. The need to learn the skills of collegiality applies equally, I suspect, to men and women. Preaching is finally a lonely task, and most of us feel rather protective about our performance in this regard. Homiletics class is a natural place for establishing some more productive habits, such as openness to learning from another's strengths and taking responsibility for helping colleagues to identify and work to overcome weaknesses. The class may need to plan some exercises which will help students to identify their points of resistance to collegiality, and in the process men and women may be able to explore the game playing and lack of trust that in the past has corrupted their dialogue. Processing the classroom dynamics may also be helpful. For instance, do men resist hearing women in the classroom and in the pulpit because they are fed up with being told things by their wives or their mothers? Do women resist criticism when it comes from men or communicate indirectly with men because they both resent and fear male power? To what extent are the men substituting co-optation for collegiality, separating the women from one another by requiring alliances with themselves? For women, the price of their acceptance as colleagues by men often is joining in alliance with men, particularly in their use of humor, against other women. Or it may take the form of accepting men's rules, which are frequently more competition-oriented and individualistic.

Understanding these dynamics of resistance and learning to build positive collegial relationships will benefit students greatly in their professional practice. The same dynamics apply to the relationship between pastor and congregation, and apply to the relationships between men and women in the congregation. It is important to learn that collegiality includes lay persons and that preaching can be a shared moment, growing out of dialogue with groups in the church and feeding back into that dialogue. Collegiality learned in seminary will reduce each minister's professional loneliness, but it is particularly important if the isolation experienced by women pastors is to be overcome. A woman pastor who is the only one, or at best one of two or three in her judicatory, usually finds herself excluded from the ongoing dialogue among her male colleagues and has no place to go for shared feedback and critique as she seeks to develop her preaching skills. Men on their part often express anger and frustration that their former all-male clergy support group has been invaded and changed by the presence of women. In seminaries, and particularly in the homiletics class, we have the opportunity for men and women to learn to be colleagues in ministry.

As men and women learn to preach they will find themselves better equipped to live and worship with the congregations they are sent to serve, which after all include men and women. The dynamics which they need to confront in the classroom are the same dynamics as will be at work in their congregations. Women and men who are pastors need to meet these dynamics with the confidence that comes from having recognized them and learned to deal with them in themselves. Men who are pastors can do a great deal to prepare a congregation to receive the ministry of a woman, and vice versa. If as preachers women and men do not put unnecessary stumbling blocks in the way of their hearers, but witness to the true Stone of stumbling, upon which we are all broken for the sake of the wholeness which only God can give, they will bring good news indeed.

NOTES

1. Mary Daly, *Beyond God the Father: Toward a Philosophy of Women's Liberation* (Boston: Beacon Press, 1973), p. 30.
2. Ibid., p. 16.